Santa

RAND McNALLY

AROUND THE WORLD

An Atlas of Maps and Pictures

Rand McNally
for
Kids

RAND McNALLY

AROUND THE WORLD

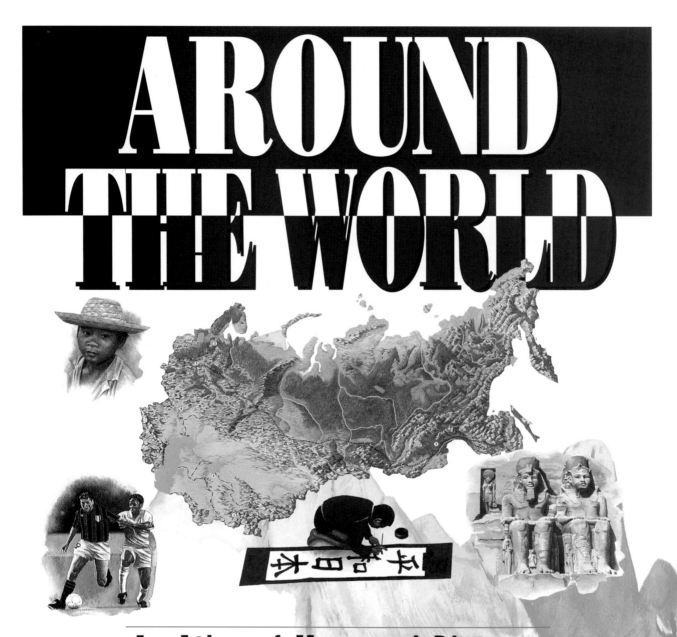

An Atlas of Maps and Pictures

Around the World
An Atlas of Maps and Pictures

Published by Rand McNally in 1994 in the USA

Copyright © 1994 Orpheus Books Ltd.

Text by Nicholas Harris
Illustrated by Gary Hincks and Steve Noon *(Garden Studio)*

Created and produced by Nicholas Harris and Joanna Turner, Orpheus Books Ltd.

Printed in Belgium

Library of Congress Cataloging-in-Publication Data

Rand McNally and Company.
      Around the world : an atlas of maps and
      pictures.
            p. cm.
      At head of title: Rand McNally.
      "Rand McNally for kids."
      Includes index.
      ISBN 0-528-83691-9 : $14.95
      1. Children's atlases. [1. Atlases.] I. Title. II.
      Title:
      Rand McNally around the world.
      G1021.R14 1994 <G&M>
      912–dc20
                                    94-9997
                                    CIP
                                    MAP AC

KEY TO ILLUSTRATIONS

Top Cheese-porters, Alkmaar market, The Netherlands *Right-hand page, top* Elephant mask, Cameroon *center* Royal palace, Bangkok, Thailand *bottom* Machu Picchu, Peru *Along bottom of page* The Kremlin, Moscow, Russia

CONTENTS

ABBREVIATIONS AND SYMBOLS
USED IN THIS BOOK

Br.	(Great) Britain
Fr.	France
ft	feet
I.	Island
Is.	Islands
km	kilometers
L.	Lake
mi	miles
Mt.	Mount
Mts.	Mountains
Neths.	Netherlands
Pop.	Population
Port.	Portugal
Rep.	Republic
sq mi	square miles
U.S.	United States
★	National capital
④	Numbers in circles show where the subjects illustrated can be found on the maps

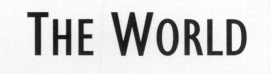

THE WORLD

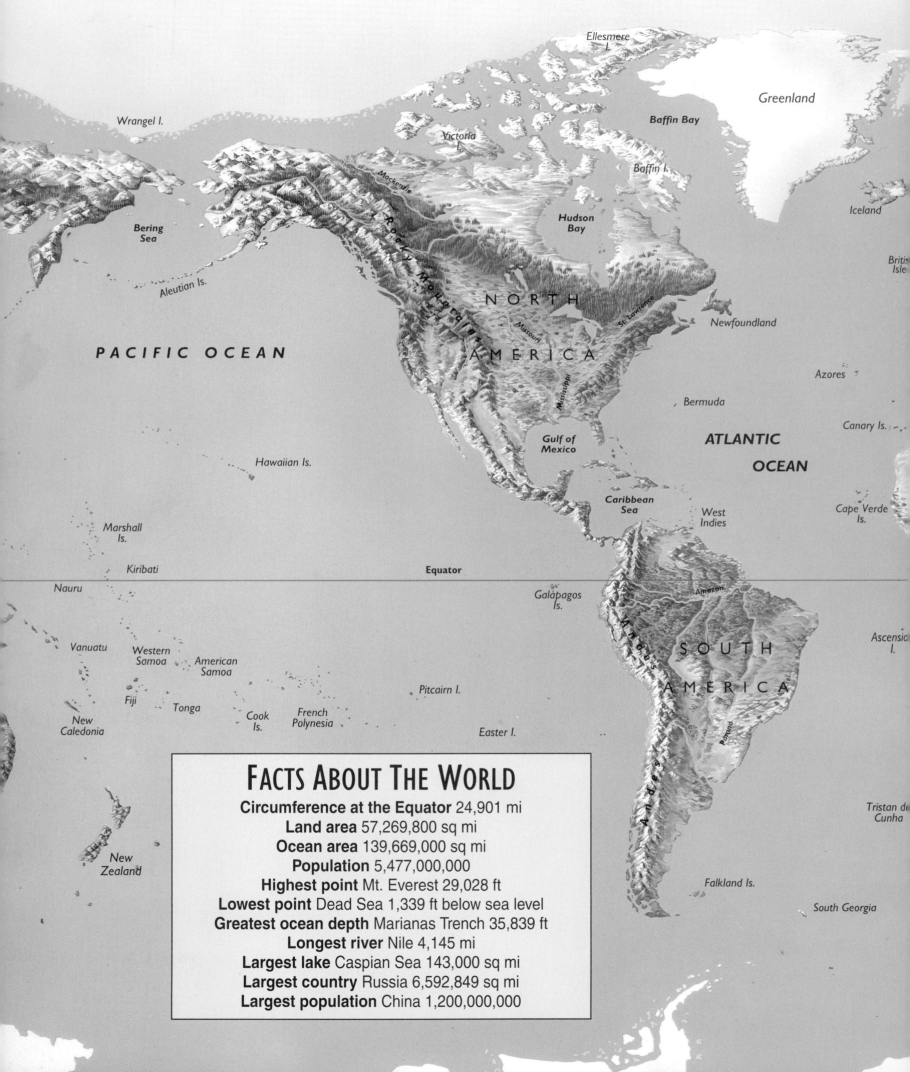

Ellesmere I.

Greenland

Wrangel I.

Baffin Bay

Victoria

Baffin I.

Iceland

Mackenzie

Bering Sea

Hudson Bay

Britis Isle

Rocky Mountains

NORTH

St. Lawrence

Aleutian Is.

AMERICA

Missouri

Newfoundland

PACIFIC OCEAN

Mississippi

Azores

Bermuda

ATLANTIC

Hawaiian Is.

Gulf of Mexico

OCEAN

Canary Is.

Caribbean Sea

West Indies

Cape Verde Is.

Marshall Is.

Kiribati

Equator

Galápagos Is.

Amazon

Nauru

Ascensio I.

Vanuatu

Western Samoa

American Samoa

SOUTH

Fiji

Tonga

Cook Is.

French Polynesia

Pitcairn I.

AMERICA

New Caledonia

Easter I.

Andes

Panamá

FACTS ABOUT THE WORLD

Circumference at the Equator 24,901 mi
Land area 57,269,800 sq mi
Ocean area 139,669,000 sq mi
Population 5,477,000,000
Highest point Mt. Everest 29,028 ft
Lowest point Dead Sea 1,339 ft below sea level
Greatest ocean depth Marianas Trench 35,839 ft
Longest river Nile 4,145 mi
Largest lake Caspian Sea 143,000 sq mi
Largest country Russia 6,592,849 sq mi
Largest population China 1,200,000,000

New Zealand

Tristan de Cunha

Falkland Is.

South Georgia

ARCTIC OCEAN

Svalbard

Severnaya Zemlya

Novaya Zemlya

Norwegian Sea

Ob

Yenisey

Lena

North Sea

Sea of Okhotsk

EUROPE

Irtysh

Volga

G o b i

Amur

Kuril Is.

Black Sea

Caspian Sea

A S I A

Honshu

Mediterranean Sea

▼ **Dead Sea**

Himalayas

▲ **Mt. Everest**

Yangtze

PACIFIC

OCEAN

S a h a r a

Nile

Arabian Sea

Bay of Bengal

South China Sea

Northern Mariana Is.

Marshall Is.

Niger

AFRICA

Philippine Is.

▼ **Marianas Trench**

Palau

Maldive Is.

Borneo

Gulf of Guinea

Zaire

Kiribati

Sumatra

New Guinea

Nauru

Seychelles

Java

Solomon Is.

Tuvalu

Cocos I.

Madagascar

INDIAN

Vanuatu

Fiji

St. Helena

Mauritius

OCEAN

Réunion

AUSTRALIA

New Caledonia

North Island

Tasman Sea

Kerguelen

South Island

SOUTHERN OCEAN

ANTARCTICA

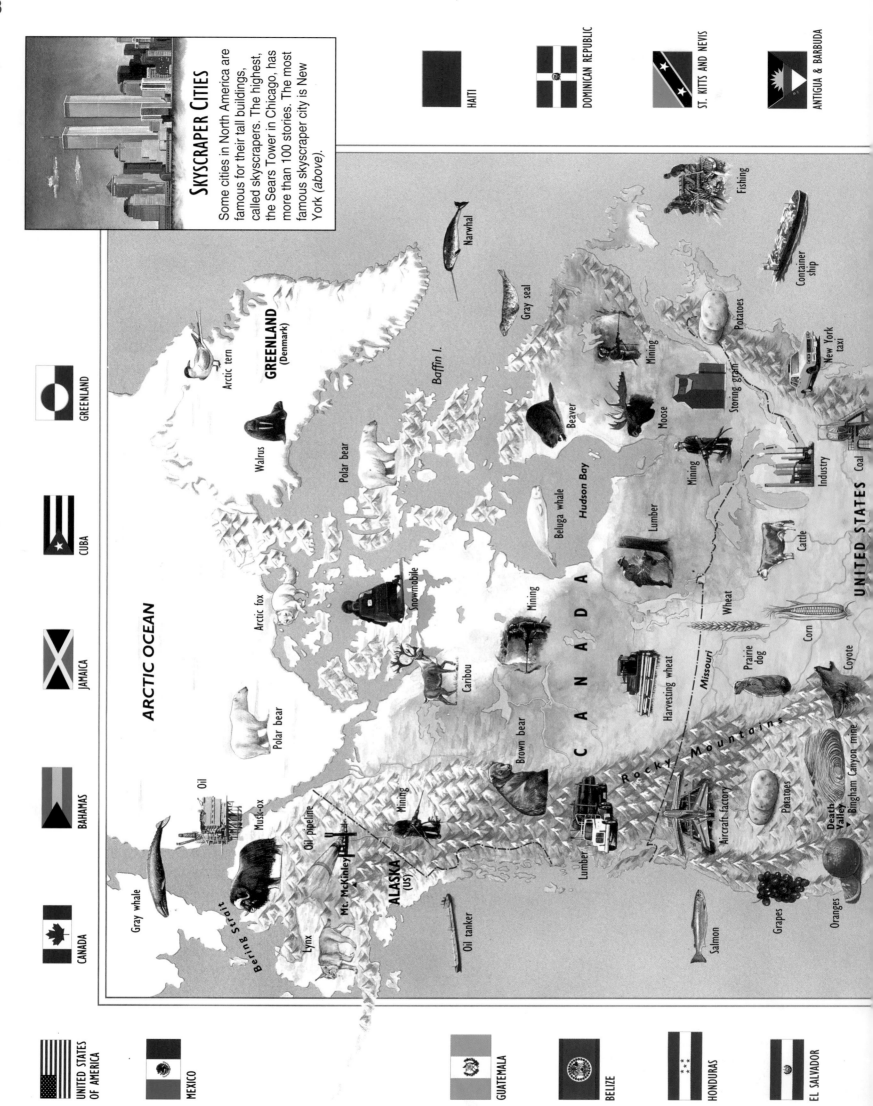

8

HAITI

DOMINICAN REPUBLIC

ST. KITTS AND NEVIS

ANTIGUA & BARBUDA

GREENLAND

CUBA

JAMAICA

BAHAMAS

CANADA

UNITED STATES OF AMERICA

MEXICO

GUATEMALA

BELIZE

HONDURAS

EL SALVADOR

ARCTIC OCEAN

GREENLAND
(Denmark)

Narwhal

Gray seal

Fishing

Container ship

Potatoes

New York taxi

Arctic tern

Baffin I.

Mining

Storing grain

Walrus

Polar bear

Beaver

Moose

Mining

Industry

Hudson Bay

Mining

Lumber

Cattle

UNITED STATES

Coal

Beluga whale

Arctic fox

Snowmobile

Wheat

Corn

Polar bear

Mining

Harvesting wheat

Missouri

Prairie dog

Coyote

Caribou

Brown bear

Rocky Mountains

Oil

Musk-ox

Oil pipeline

Mining

Lumber

Aircraft factory

Potatoes

Death Valley

Bingham Canyon mine

Gray whale

Bering Strait

Mt. McKinley

ALASKA
(US)

Grapes

Oranges

Lynx

Oil tanker

Salmon

CANADA

NORTH AMERICA

NORTH AMERICA stretches from the icy Arctic islands of Greenland and northern Canada to the hot, steamy rain forests of the Caribbean coast.

Human beings first arrived in North America from Asia, possibly about 12,000 years ago. It was the time of Ice Ages when ice sheets covered large parts of the world. The Bering Strait, which separates North America from Asia, was then dry land. The first Americans spread out across the continent and lived by hunting the animals they found there.

The first Europeans to set eyes on North America were Norsemen. About 1,000 years ago, they settled in Newfoundland. After Christopher Columbus' voyage of discovery in 1492, Spanish, English, and French explorers began to travel inland.

FACTS ABOUT NORTH AMERICA

Area 9,500,000 sq mi
Population 438,200,000
Highest point Mt. McKinley (Alaska, USA) 20,320 ft
Lowest point Death Valley (USA) 282 ft below sea level
Longest river Mississippi-Missouri (USA) 3,710 mi
Largest lake Superior (Canada and USA) 31,700 sq mi
Largest country Canada 3,849,674 sq mi
Largest population United States of America 256,420,000
Largest city Mexico City (Mexico) 8,831,000

PACIFIC OCEAN

ATLANTIC OCEAN

CARIBBEAN SEA

GULF OF MEXICO

SOUTH AMERICA

Mississippi

MEXICO

CUBA

BAHAMAS

PUERTO RICO (US)

DOMINICAN REP.

HAITI

JAMAICA

BELIZE

GUATEMALA

HONDURAS

EL SALVADOR

NICARAGUA

COSTA RICA

PANAMA

TRINIDAD AND TOBAGO

Kangaroo rat
Brown pelicans diving
Sidewinder
Mining
Harvesting wheat
Herding cattle
Soybeans
Gas
Cotton
Tobacco
Alligator
Shrimps
Space Shuttle launch
Corn
Oil
Coffee
Toucan
Bananas
Cutting sugar cane
Mining
Cocoa
Tourism
Panama Canal

NICARAGUA
COSTA RICA
PANAMA
TRINIDAD & TOBAGO
GRENADA
ST. VINCENT AND THE GRENADINES
BARBADOS
ST. LUCIA
DOMINICA

NATIONS OF NORTH AMERICA

ANGUILLA
Area 35 sq mi **Population** 8,960
Capital The Valley **Language** English

ANTIGUA and **BARBUDA**
Area 171 sq mi **Population** 66,000
Capital St. John's **Language** English

BAHAMAS
Area 5,382 sq mi **Pop.** 258,000
Capital Nassau **Language** English

BARBADOS
Area 166 sq mi **Population** 255,000
Capital Bridgetown **Language**
English

BELIZE
Area 8,866 sq mi **Population**
170,000 **Capital** Belmopan
Languages English, Spanish

BERMUDA
Area 21 sq mi **Population** 59,000
Capital Hamilton **Language** English

BRITISH VIRGIN ISLANDS
Area 59 sq mi **Population** 17,000
Capital Road Town **Language**
English

CANADA
Area 3,849,674 sq mi **Population**
27,409,000 **Capital** Ottawa
Languages English, French

COSTA RICA
Area 19,730 sq mi **Population**
3,064,000 **Capital** San José
Language Spanish

CUBA
Area 42,804 sq mi **Pop.** 10,736,000
Capital Havana **Language** Spanish

DOMINICA
Area 305 sq mi **Pop.** 72,000 **Capital**
Roseau **Languages** English, Creole

DOMINICAN REPUBLIC
Area 18,704 sq mi **Population**
7,321,000 **Capital** Santo Domingo
Language Spanish

EL SALVADOR
Area 8,124 sq mi **Population**
5,376,000 **Capital** San Salvador
Language Spanish

GREENLAND
Area 840,004 sq mi **Population** 57,000
Capital Godthåb **Languages** Inuit,
Danish

GRENADA
Area 133 sq mi **Population** 98,000
Capital St. George's **Languages** English,
French patois

GUADELOUPE
Area 687 sq mi **Population** 387,000
Capital Basse-Terre **Languages** French,
Creole

GUATEMALA
Area 42,042 sq mi **Population** 9,745,000
Capital Guatemala **Language** Spanish

HAITI
Area 10,714 sq mi **Population** 6,625,000
Capital Port-au-Prince **Languages**
French, Creole

▲ Hutterite girl, from
Canada. The Hutterites are
devout Christians who live
in small communities on the
Great Plains of Canada.
Originally from Ukraine,
they wear old-fashioned
clothes and speak their own
language, German, among
themselves. ②

▲ Inuit (Eskimo) boy ①

▲ Hopi girl, from the United States ⑥

HONDURAS
Area 43,277 sq mi **Population** 4,916,000
Capital Tegucigalpa **Language** Spanish

JAMAICA
Area 4,244 sq mi **Population** 2,461,000
Capital Kingston **Language** English

MARTINIQUE (Fr.)
Area 425 sq mi **Population** 360,000
Capital Fort-de-France **Languages**
French, Creole

MEXICO
Area 759,534 sq mi **Pop.** 87,836,000
Capital Mexico City **Language** Spanish

MONTSERRAT
Area 40 sq mi **Population** 11,000
Capital Plymouth **Language** English

NETHERLANDS ANTILLES
Area 309 sq mi **Population** 189,000
Capital Willemstad **Languages** Dutch,
Papiamento

NICARAGUA
Area 50,054 sq mi **Population**
3,999,000 **Capital** Managua
Languages Spanish, English

PANAMA
Area 29,157 sq mi **Population**
2,315,000 **Capital** Panama
Language Spanish

PUERTO RICO
Area 3,515 sq mi **Population**
3,522,000 **Capital** San Juan
Languages Spanish, English

ST. KITTS AND NEVIS
Area 104 sq mi **Population** 44,000
Capital Basseterre **Language**
English

ST. LUCIA
Area 238 sq mi **Population** 153,000
Capital Castries **Languages** English,
French patois

ST. VINCENT AND THE GRENADINES
Area 150 sq mi **Population** 117,000
Capital Kingstown **Language** English

TRINIDAD AND TOBAGO
Area 1,980 sq mi **Pop.** 1,253,000
Capital Port of Spain **Languages**
English, French, Spanish, Hindi,
Chinese

UNITED STATES OF AMERICA
Area 3,787,425 sq mi **Population**
256,420,000 **Capital** Washington,
D.C. **Languages** English, Spanish

US VIRGIN ISLANDS
Area 137 sq mi **Population** 102,000
Capital Charlotte Amalie **Languages**
English, Spanish, Creole

▲ Guatemalan girl ⑤

▲ Boy from the Caribbean islands ④

▲ American boy ③

A VIRGIN IS. (Br. & US)
B ST. MARTIN (Fr. & Neths.)
C ANGUILLA (Br.)
D ST. KITTS AND NEVIS
E ANTIGUA AND BARBUDA
F GUADELOUPE (Fr.)
G DOMINICA
H MARTINIQUE (Fr.)
I ST. LUCIA
J ST. VINCENT AND THE
   GRENADINES
K BARBADOS
L GRENADA

ATLANTIC OCEAN

BOSTON
NEW YORK
PHILADELPHIA
WASHINGTON, D.C.
BALTIMORE
CLEVELAND
CINCINNATI
ATLANTA
TORONTO
L. Ontario
L. Erie
DETROIT
L. Michigan
CHICAGO
MILWAUKEE
MINNEAPOLIS
ST. LOUIS
KANSAS CITY
DALLAS
HOUSTON
NEW ORLEANS
MIAMI
DENVER
Colorado
Snake
SALT LAKE CITY
PHOENIX
SAN FRANCISCO
LOS ANGELES
SAN DIEGO
MEXICALI

UNITED STATES

Mississippi
Ohio
Arkansas

BAHAMAS
NASSAU
CUBA
HAVANA
JAMAICA
KINGSTON
HAITI
PORT-AU-PRINCE
DOMINICAN REPUBLIC
SANTO DOMINGO
SAN JUAN
PUERTO RICO (U.S.)
NETHS. ANTILLES
TRINIDAD AND TOBAGO
PORT OF SPAIN

CARIBBEAN SEA

Gulf of Mexico

MÉRIDA
VILLAHERMOSA
MEXICO CITY
GUADALAJARA
MONTERREY
Rio Grande

MEXICO

Gulf of California

PACIFIC OCEAN

BELIZE
BELMOPAN
GUATEMALA
GUATEMALA
SAN SALVADOR
EL SALVADOR
TEGUCIGALPA
HONDURAS
NICARAGUA
MANAGUA
SAN JOSÉ
COSTA RICA
PANAMA
PANAMA

Scale
0   800 km
0   500 mi

★ National capital
☆ Other capital

See pages 16-17 for state names and
capitals in the United States of America

CANADA

CANADA is the second largest country in the world, after Russia. It is a land of high, snow-capped mountains in the west, forests and lakes in the center, and frozen, treeless wastes in the Arctic north. Canada's cities and farmland are located in the south, close to the border with the United States.

▲ This is the face of a bear. You can see its wild eyes, fearsome teeth, and flared nostrils! It was carved on a totem pole by Native Americans from British Columbia. Each pole has several carvings, one on top of the other. ⑥

◄ The wheat fields of Alberta and Saskatchewan are known as the "prairies." The harvested grain is stored in grain elevators like these. ①

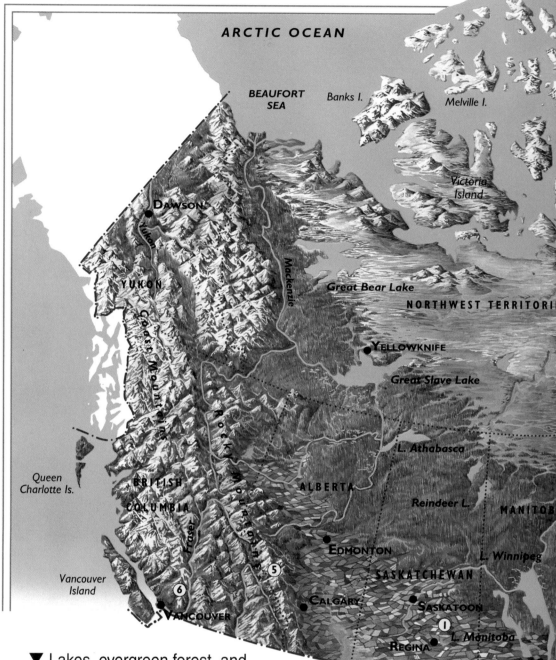

▼ Lakes, evergreen forest, and snowy peaks fill this view of a valley in the Rocky Mountains. ⑤

◀ A fishing boat winds in its nets. Usually, fishing vessels are everywhere in the Gulf of St. Lawrence and off the coast of Newfoundland. The stocks of cod and herring in these shallow seas have fallen dramatically. ②

▲ Ice hockey is one of Canada's most popular sports. Nearly every town has an ice rink and a local team. The biggest prize of the season, the Stanley Cup, has been won most often by the Montréal Canadiens. Even many of the players on the United States teams are Canadian. ③

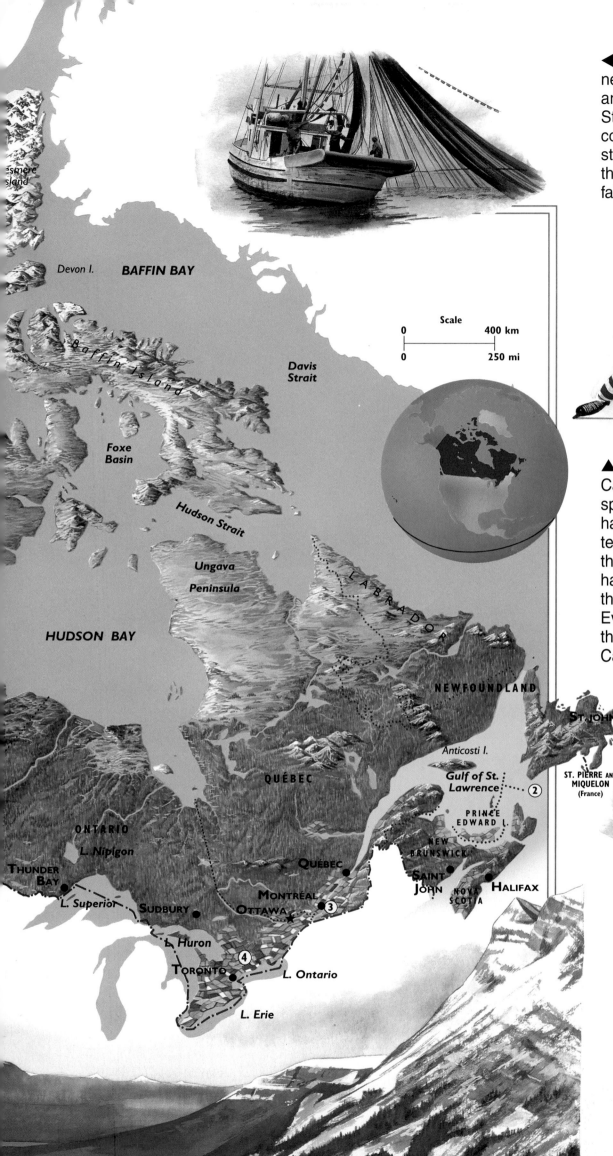

Scale
0   400 km
0   250 mi

Devon I. **BAFFIN BAY**

Davis Strait

Baffin Island

Foxe Basin

Hudson Strait

Ungava Peninsula

LABRADOR

HUDSON BAY

NEWFOUNDLAND

ST. JOHN'S

Anticosti I.

QUÉBEC

Gulf of St. Lawrence ②

ST. PIERRE AND MIQUELON (France)

PRINCE EDWARD I.

ONTARIO

L. Nipigon

THUNDER BAY

L. Superior

SUDBURY

QUÉBEC

MONTRÉAL

OTTAWA ③

NEW BRUNSWICK

SAINT JOHN

NOVA SCOTIA

HALIFAX

L. Huron

④

TORONTO

L. Ontario

L. Erie

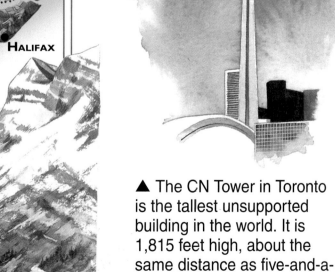

▲ The CN Tower in Toronto is the tallest unsupported building in the world. It is 1,815 feet high, about the same distance as five-and-a-half football fields placed end to end! ④

UNITED STATES OF AMERICA

VT.	VERMONT
N.H.	NEW HAMPSHIRE
MASS.	MASSACHUSETTS
CONN.	CONNECTICUT
R.I.	RHODE ISLAND
N.J.	NEW JERSEY
MD.	MARYLAND
DEL.	DELAWARE

THE UNITED STATES of America consists of 50 states, including Hawaii and Alaska.

East of the Rocky Mountains, vast farmlands stretch away as far as the eye can see. Sprawling cities cluster together in the north-eastern states. West of the Rockies, much of the land inland from the Pacific coast is desert.

▲ The trunk of this giant sequoia tree in California is so thick, cars can drive through it! One tree of this kind, known as "General Sherman," is the most massive living thing in the world. ⑥

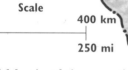

▼ Much of the southwestern USA is desert. Some spectacular landscapes, like Monument Valley in Arizona, are found here. ⑤

Scale
0 — 400 km
0 — 250 mi

ALASKA
ANCHORAGE
Aleutian Is.

Scale
0 — 600 km
0 — 500 mi

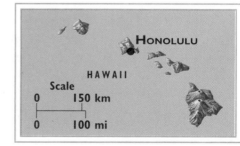

HONOLULU
HAWAII
Scale
0 — 150 km
0 — 100 mi

◀ The Golden Gate Bridge crosses the entrance to San Francisco Bay. Sometimes fog from the Pacific rolls in beneath it. ①

◀ The Gateway Arch, in St. Louis, Missouri, is the tallest monument in the world. It was built to mark the city's historic role as "gateway to the West." Wagon trains once set out from here on their way to California. The Arch is hollow: inside, elevators go up to a viewing platform at the top. ②

▲ The United States Capitol in Washington, D.C., is one of the most famous landmarks in the world. Congress, which consists of the House of Representatives and the Senate, meets inside this building. ③

▲ This is a club in New Orleans, Louisiana, where jazz musicians are performing. New Orleans is the home of jazz, a style of music invented by black musicians in the early years of the twentieth century. The particular kind of jazz played here is known as Dixieland, a name sometimes given to the southern states of America. ④

STATES OF THE U.S.

ALABAMA
Area 52,423 sq mi **Population** 4,128,000
Capital Montgomery **Largest city** Birmingham

ALASKA
Area 656,424 sq mi **Population** 564,000
Capital Juneau **Largest city** Anchorage

ARIZONA
Area 114,006 sq mi **Pop.** 3,872,000
Capital and largest city Phoenix

ARKANSAS
Area 53,182 sq mi **Population** 2,410,000
Capital and largest city Little Rock

CALIFORNIA
Area 163,707 sq mi **Pop.** 31,310,000
Capital Sacramento **Largest city** Los Angeles

COLORADO
Area 104,100 sq mi **Pop.** 3,410,000
Capital and largest city Denver

CONNECTICUT
Area 5,544 sq mi **Population** 3,358,000
Capital Hartford **Largest city** Bridgeport

▲ Bucking bronco at a rodeo ⑥

DELAWARE
Area 2,489 sq mi **Population** 692,000
Capital Dover **Largest city** Wilmington

FLORIDA
Area 65,758 sq mi **Pop.** 13,630,000
Capital Tallahassee **Largest city** Jacksonville

GEORGIA
Area 59,441 sq mi **Population** 6,795,000
Capital and largest city Atlanta

HAWAII
Area 10,932 sq mi **Population** 1,159,000
Capital and largest city Honolulu

IDAHO
Area 83,574 sq mi **Population** 1,026,000
Capital and largest city Boise

ILLINOIS
Area 57,918 sq mi **Population** 11,640,000
Capital Springfield **Largest city** Chicago

INDIANA
Area 36,420 sq mi **Pop.** 5,667,000
Capital and largest city Indianapolis

IOWA
Area 56,276 sq mi **Pop.** 2,821,000
Capital and largest city Des Moines

KANSAS
Area 82,282 sq mi **Pop.** 2,539,000
Capital Topeka **Largest city** Wichita

KENTUCKY
Area 40,411 sq mi **Pop.** 3,745,000
Capital Frankfort **Largest city** Louisville

LOUISIANA
Area 51,843 sq mi **Pop.** 4,282,000
Capital Baton Rouge **Largest city** New Orleans

MAINE
Area 35,387 sq mi **Pop.** 1,257,000
Capital Augusta **Largest city** Portland

MARYLAND
Area 12,407 sq mi **Pop.** 4,975,000
Capital Annapolis **Largest city** Baltimore

MASSACHUSETTS
Area 10,555 sq mi **Pop.** 6,103,000
Capital and largest city Boston

MICHIGAN
Area 96,810 sq mi **Population** 9,488,000 **Capital** Lansing **Largest city** Detroit

▶ Hoover Dam ①

▶ Cliff Palace, built by Pueblo Native Americans about 800 years ago ⑤

MINNESOTA
Area 86,943 sq mi **Population** 4,513,000 **Capital** St. Paul **Largest city** Minneapolis

MISSISSIPPI
Area 48,434 sq mi **Population** 2,616,000 **Capital and largest city** Jackson

▲ The Fall in New England ②

NEW MEXICO
Area 121,598 sq mi **Population** 1,590,000 **Capital** Santa Fe **Largest city** Albuquerque

NEW YORK
Area 54,475 sq mi **Population** 18,350,000 **Capital** Albany **Largest city** New York

NORTH CAROLINA
Area 53,821 sq mi **Population** 6,846,000 **Capital** Raleigh **Largest city** Charlotte

NORTH DAKOTA
Area 70,704 sq mi **Population** 632,000 **Capital** Bismarck **Largest city** Fargo

OHIO
Area 44,828 sq mi **Pop.** 11,025,000 **Capital and largest city** Columbus

OKLAHOMA
Area 69,903 sq mi **Population** 3,205,000 **Capital and largest city** Oklahoma City

OREGON
Area 96,386 sq mi **Population** 2,949,000 **Capital** Salem **Largest city** Portland

PENNSYLVANIA
Area 46,058 sq mi **Pop.** 12,105,000 **Capital** Harrisburg **Largest city** Philadelphia

RHODE ISLAND
Area 1,545 sq mi **Population** 1,026,000 **Capital and largest city** Providence

SOUTH CAROLINA
Area 32,007 sq mi **Population** 3,616,000 **Capital and largest city** Columbia

SOUTH DAKOTA
Area 77,121 sq mi **Population** 718,000 **Capital** Pierre **Largest city** Sioux Falls

TENNESSEE
Area 42,146 sq mi **Population** 5,026,000 **Capital** Nashville **Largest city** Memphis

TEXAS
Area 268,601 sq mi **Pop.** 17,610,000 **Capital** Austin **Largest city** Houston

UTAH
Area 84,904 sq mi **Population** 1,795,000 **Capital and largest city** Salt Lake City

VT.   VERMONT
N.H. NEW HAMPSHIRE
CONN. CONNECTICUT
R.I. RHODE ISLAND
N.J. NEW JERSEY
DEL. DELAWARE
MD.   MARYLAND

★ **National capital**
☆ **State capital**

ATLANTIC OCEAN

▲ Whale-watching off the Atlantic coast ③

VERMONT
Area 9,615 sq mi **Population** 590,000 **Capital** Montpelier **Largest city** Burlington

VIRGINIA
Area 42,769 sq mi **Population** 6,411,000 **Capital** Richmond **Largest city** Virginia Beach

WASHINGTON
Area 71,303 sq mi **Population** 5,052,000 **Capital** Olympia **Largest city** Seattle

WEST VIRGINIA
Area 24,231 sq mi **Population** 1,795,000 **Capital and largest city** Charleston

WISCONSIN
Area 65,503 sq mi **Population** 5,000,000 **Capital** Madison **Largest city** Milwaukee

WYOMING
Area 97,818 sq mi **Population** 462,000 **Capital and largest city** Cheyenne

MISSOURI
Area 69,709 sq mi **Population** 5,231,000 **Capital** Jefferson City **Largest city** Kansas City

MONTANA
Area 147,046 sq mi **Population** 821,000 **Capital** Helena **Largest city** Billings

NEBRASKA
Area 77,358 sq mi **Pop.** 1,615,000 **Capital** Lincoln **Largest city** Omaha

NEVADA
Area 110,567 sq mi **Population** 1,308,000 **Capital** Carson City **Largest city** Las Vegas

NEW HAMPSHIRE
Area 9,351 sq mi **Population** 1,154,000 **Capital** Concord **Largest city** Manchester

NEW JERSEY
Area 8,722 sq mi **Pop.** 7,898,000 **Capital** Trenton **Largest city** Newark

◄ The Statue of Liberty, New York ④

MEXICO AND CENTRAL AMERICA

◄ A colorful tree frog from Central America. ①

IN NORTHERN Mexico, two mountain chains run down both coastlines. The high, flat land between them is dry and dusty, dotted with low bushes called scrub. Farther south in Central America, the land gradually narrows and the climate becomes more tropical.

▲ This is a volcano in Costa Rica. Smoke drifts gently from the crater at its summit. Sometimes, without warning, a volcano will erupt. In a huge explosion, great clouds of smoke, rock, and ash fill the sky. Lava, rock that is so hot it flows like a liquid, cascades down the mountainside. ⑥

MEXICALI

CIUDAD JUAREZ

Baja California

CULIACÁN

MONTERREY

Rio Grande

MEXICO

GULF OF MEXICO

GUADALAJARA

Yucatán Peninsula

MÉRID

⑤

MEXICO CITY ★

VERACRUZ

VILLAHERMOSA

Scale

0   600 km
0   400 mi

BEL

BELMOPAN ★

GUATEMALA

GUATEMALA ★ TEGUCIGAL

SAN SALVADOR ★

EL SALVADOR

◀ The Panama Canal is a man-made water link between the Caribbean Sea and the Pacific Ocean. Ships pass through locks with the help of little railroad locomotives. ②

◀ The waters around the islands in the Caribbean Sea are warm and full of wildlife. Close to shore lie coral reefs, natural undersea banks built up by tiny animals. People dive underwater to see the amazing shapes and colors, and watch many kinds of fish swim by. ③

▲ These women from Haiti are winnowing rice. They shake the grains through a sieve. The part of the rice that is good to eat falls to the ground, while the husks are left in the sieve. ④

▼ Before Europeans arrived in Central America, the Native Americans had the land to themselves. The Maya made clearings in the rain forest and built great cities. Most of these cities, like Chichén Itzá, pictured below, are dominated by a large central pyramid. ⑤

LESSER ANTILLES

A VIRGIN IS. (Br. & U.S.)
B ST. MARTIN (France & Neths)
C ANGUILLA (Br.)
D ST. KITTS AND NEVIS
E ANTIGUA AND BARBUDA
F GUADELOUPE (France)
G DOMINICA
H MARTINIQUE (France)
I ST. LUCIA
J ST. VINCENT AND THE GRENADINES
K BARBADOS
L GRENADA
M TRINIDAD AND TOBAGO
N NETHERLANDS ANTILLES (Neths)

BAHAMAS

HAVANA

CUBA

JAMAICA

KINGSTON

HAITI

PORT-AU-PRINCE

DOMINICAN REPUBLIC

SANTO DOMINGO

Hispaniola

SAN JUAN

PUERTO RICO (U.S.)

HONDURAS

NICARAGUA

MANAGUA

CARIBBEAN SEA

COSTA RICA

SAN JOSÉ

PANAMA

PANAMA

BRAZIL

ECUADOR

PERU

BOLIVIA

PARAGUAY

URUGUAY

ARGENTINA

CHILE

FRENCH GUIANA

SURINAME

GUYANA

VENEZUELA

COLOMBIA

SOUTH AMERICA

SOUTH AMERICA reaches from the tropical coast of the Caribbean to the icy seas of the Southern Ocean. It is joined to North America by a thin neck of land, the isthmus of Panama. Most of South America's population lives in the east of the continent. Apart from the Guianas and Brazil (where Portuguese is spoken) Spanish is the main language. Much of South America was once under Spanish rule. The people themselves are descended from the Native Americans, Spanish and Portuguese settlers, later immigrants from other parts of Europe, and Africans.

FACTS ABOUT SOUTH AMERICA

Area 6,820,000 sq mi
Population 310,700,000
Highest point Aconcagua (Argentina) 22,834 ft
Lowest point Salinas Chicas (Argentina) 138 ft below sea level
Longest river Amazon 4,007 mi
Largest lake Titicaca (Peru and Bolivia) 3,220 sq mi
Largest country Brazil 3,286,500 sq mi
Largest population Brazil 153,322,000
Largest city São Paulo (Brazil) 10,063,110

▲ Native American girl, from the Amazon region of Brazil ①

▲ Native American girl from the Andes, Bolivia ③

ATLANTIC OCEAN

Equator

Manatee

Sugar cane

Bananas

Cocoa

Vampire bat

Mining

Armadillo

Mining

B R A Z I L

Piranha

Capybara

Mining

Hummingbird

Amazon

Anaconda

Spider monkey

Jaguar

BOLIVIA

FRENCH GUIANA

SURINAME

GUYANA

VENEZUELA

Cattle

Oil

Giant anteater

COLOMBIA

Sloth

Coffee

Cocoa

ECUADOR

Andes

P E R U

Potatoes

Mining

Fishing

NATIONS OF SOUTH AMERICA

ARGENTINA
Area 1,073,519 sq mi **Pop.** 32,370,000
Capital Buenos Aires **Language** Spanish

BOLIVIA
Area 424,165 sq mi **Pop.** 7,612,000
Capitals La Paz, Sucre **Languages** Spanish, Quechua, Aymara

BRAZIL
Area 3,286,500 sq mi **Population** 153,322,000 **Capital** Brasília **Language** Portuguese

CHILE
Area 292,135 sq mi **Pop.** 13,599,000
Capital Santiago **Language** Spanish

COLOMBIA
Area 440,831 sq mi **Population** 32,841,000 **Capital** Bogotá **Language** Spanish

ECUADOR
Area 109,484 sq mi **Population** 11,078,000 **Capital** Quito **Languages** Spanish, Quechua

FALKLAND ISLANDS
Area 4,700 sq mi **Population** 2,000
Capital Stanley **Language** English

FRENCH GUIANA
Area 35,135 sq mi **Population** 115,000
Capital Cayenne **Languages** French, Creole

GUYANA
Area 83,000 sq mi **Population** 740,000
Capital Georgetown **Languages** English, Hindi, Urdu

PARAGUAY
Area 157,048 sq mi **Population** 4,397,000 **Capital** Asunción **Languages** Spanish, Guarani

PERU
Area 496,225 sq mi **Population** 22,332,000 **Capital** Lima **Languages** Spanish, Quechua, Aymara

SURINAME
Area 63,251 sq mi **Population** 400,000 **Capital** Paramaribo **Languages** Dutch, Hindi, Javanese

URUGUAY
Area 68,500 sq mi **Population** 3,094,000 **Capital** Montevideo **Language** Spanish

VENEZUELA
Area 352,145 sq mi **Population** 20,226,000 **Capital** Caracas **Language** Spanish

▲ Chilean boy ②

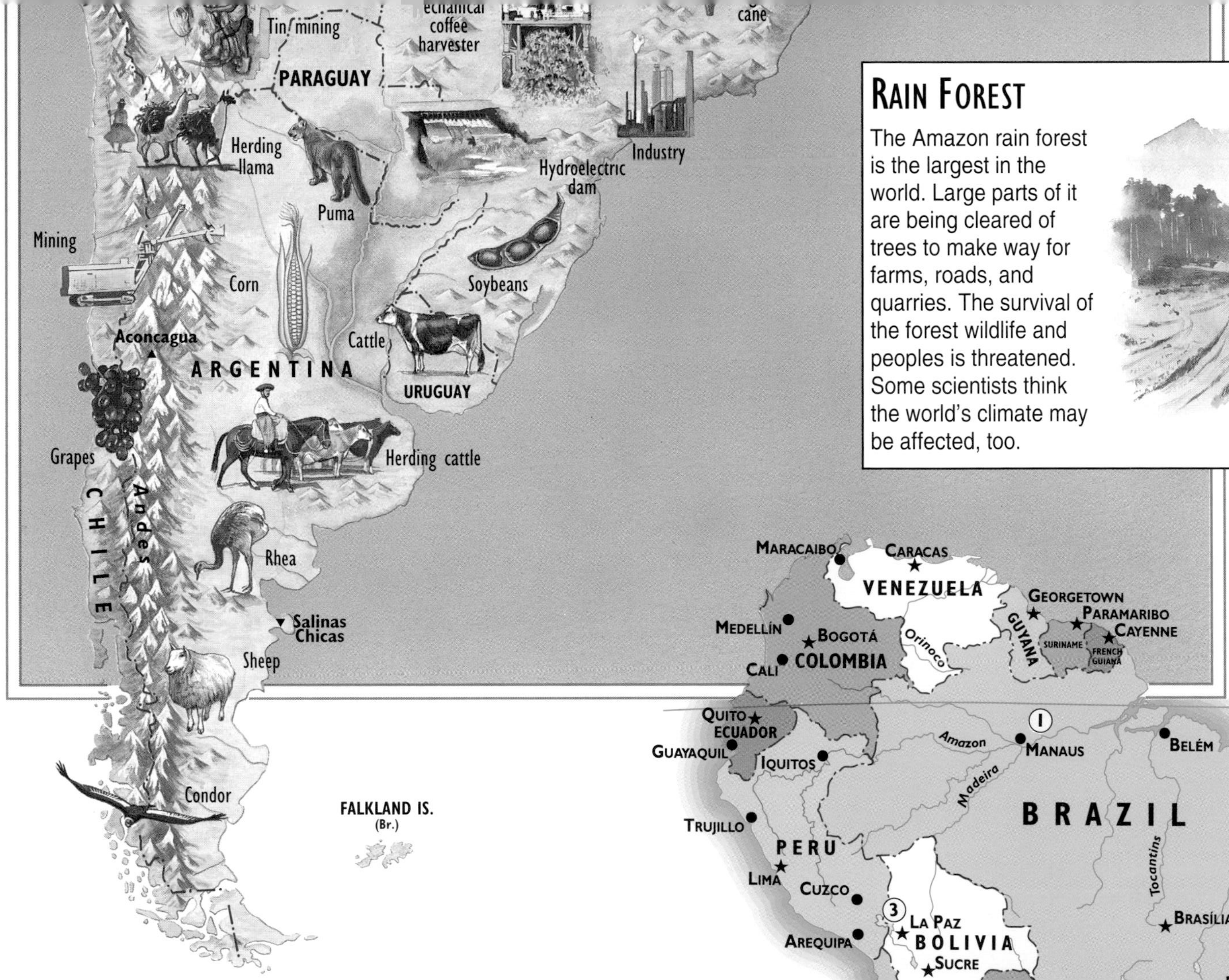

RAIN FOREST

The Amazon rain forest is the largest in the world. Large parts of it are being cleared of trees to make way for farms, roads, and quarries. The survival of the forest wildlife and peoples is threatened. Some scientists think the world's climate may be affected, too.

Scale 1000 km
        750 mi

★ National capital

FALKLAND IS. (Br.)

Equator

Map labels: RECIFE, FORTALEZA, SALVADOR, BELO HORIZONTE, RIO DE JANEIRO, SÃO PAULO, BRASÍLIA, PORTO ALEGRE, BELÉM, BRAZIL, Tocantins, GEORGETOWN, PARAMARIBO, CAYENNE, SURINAME, FRENCH GUIANA, GUYANA, MANAUS, MONTEVIDEO, BUENOS AIRES, URUGUAY, ASUNCIÓN, PARAGUAY, ROSARIO, BAHIA BLANCA, CARACAS, VENEZUELA, Orinoco, Amazon, Madeira, Paraná, LA PAZ, BOLIVIA, SUCRE, CORDOBA, ARGENTINA, CONCEPCIÓN, BOGOTÁ, COLOMBIA, MARACAIBO, MEDELLIN, CALI, QUITO, ECUADOR, GUAYAQUIL, IQUITOS, PERU, CUZCO, LIMA, AREQUIPA, TRUJILLO, ANTOFAGASTA, VALPARAISO, SANTIAGO, CHILE, FALKLAND IS. (Br.), ① ② ③

FALKLAND IS. (Br.)

Salinas Chicas
Andes
ARGENTINA
PARAGUAY
URUGUAY
CHILE
Aconcagua

Illustration labels: cane, Industry, Hydroelectric dam, Soybeans, coffee, harvester, Cattle, Herding cattle, Tin/mining, Herding llama, Puma, Corn, Grapes, Mining, Rhea, Sheep, Condor

BRAZIL AND ITS NEIGHBORS

LYING ACROSS the center of this map is a huge river basin. It looks as if an enormous green blanket has been laid across it. This is the Amazon rain forest. Hundreds of different kinds of birds and animals live here.

Around the rim of the basin are highlands. (Turn to pages 24-25 to see a map of the Andes, the mountains which form the western edge.) Rivers flow down from them and snake through the forest to meet the mighty Amazon. This vast river carries one fifth of all the world's fresh water into the Atlantic ocean!

Few people inhabit the Amazon region. Most Brazilians live in the crowded cities of the southeast.

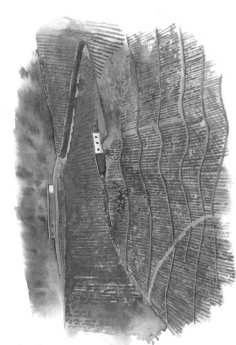

▲ Hundreds of neat rows of coffee trees wind across a hillside in Colombia. ①

▲ The Angel Falls in Venezuela are the highest in the world. ②

▲ These oil rigs are standing in the shallow waters of Lake Maracaibo, Venezuela. ⑦

▲ A scarlet macaw, a rain forest bird. ⑥

CARIBBEAN SEA

ATLANTIC OCEAN

MARACAIBO ⑦

CARACAS ★

Orinoco

V E N E Z U E L A

Guyana Highlands ②

Andes Mountains

MEDELLÍN ①

BOGOTÁ ★

CALI

C O L O M B I A

Japurá

Negro

GEORGETOWN ★

PARAMARIBO ★

CAYENNE ★

G U Y A N A

SURINAME

FRENCH GUIANA ⑤

Amazon

MANAUS

Amazon

Madeira

Xingu

B R A Z I L

BELÉM

FORTALEZA

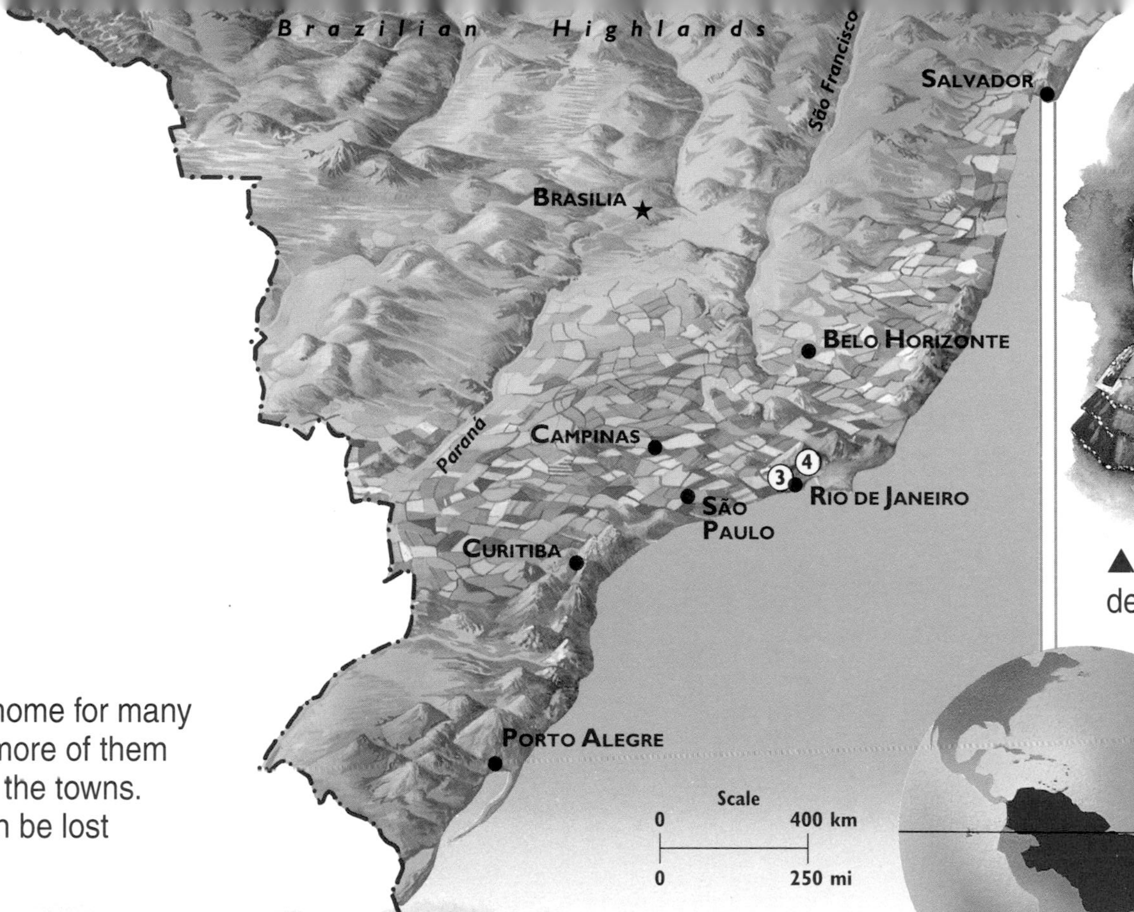

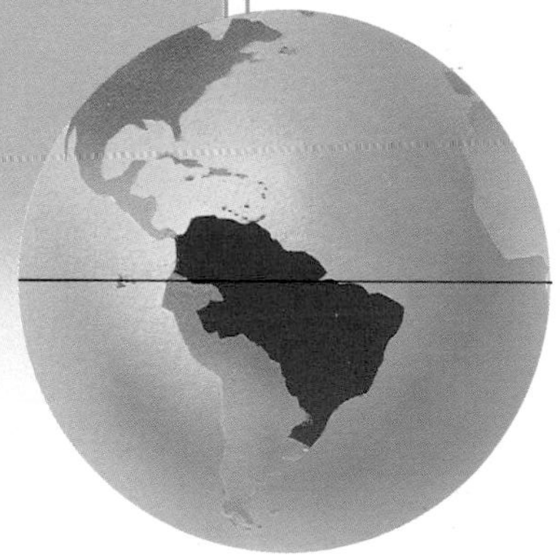

▲ A dancer at a Rio de Janeiro festival. ③

▲ The Amazon rain forest is home for many Native Americans. More and more of them are leaving to live and work in the towns. Their old ways of life may soon be lost forever. ⑤

▼ In January 1503, a Portuguese explorer named Goncalo Coelho sailed his ship into a Brazilian bay. He thought he had found the mouth of a great river, and called the bay the January River, or, in his own language, Rio de Janeiro.
A great city has since grown up around the shores of that beautiful bay. The Sugar Loaf mountain, shaped like a rounded cone, overlooks its harbor. Rich people live in apartments with wonderful views. Poor people live in shabby slums on the edge of the city. Their shantytowns are known as the *favelas*. ④

Scale
0 — 400 km
0 — 250 mi

SALVADOR
São Francisco
Brazilian Highlands
BELO HORIZONTE
BRASILIA ★
RIO DE JANEIRO ④ ③
SÃO PAULO
CAMPINAS
Paraná
CURITIBA
PORTO ALEGRE

THE ANDES

THE ANDES MOUNTAINS run from top to bottom of this map. In Ecuador, Peru, and parts of Bolivia, tropical rain forests cling to their eastern slopes. Over on the western side, where the mountains rise behind the Pacific coast like a great wall, there are not even any trees – just desert. Some parts have not felt rain for more than 400 years!

Until the Spaniards first arrived in 1524, the mighty Inca emperor reigned supreme over this land. Today, the Indians still speak Quechua, the language of the Incas. They farm the steep hillsides of the Andes and graze their llamas and alpacas on the high plains.

▲ The Spanish invaders never found Machu Picchu. This Inca city was built high in the mountains. It was "lost" to the rest of the world until 1911. ②

(above, left) For hundreds of years, people have crossed the deep gorges in the Andes by rope bridges. ①

▲ The Galápagos Islands are famous for their wildlife, like this giant tortoise. ⑦

GALÁPAGOS ISLANDS
(Ecuador) ⑦

QUITO ★
ECUADOR
GUAYAQUIL ●

IQUITOS ●
Marañón
Ucayali

P E R U

Andes Mountains

① ②
CUZCO ●
L. Titicaca
TRUJILLO ●
LIMA ★
AREQUIPA ●
IQUIQUE ●
Atacama Desert
ANTOFAGASTA ●

⑥
LA PAZ ★
B O L I V I A
SUCRE ★
SANTA CRUZ ●
⑤

Gran Chaco
PARAGUAY
Paraguay
ASUNCIÓN ★
TUCUMÁN

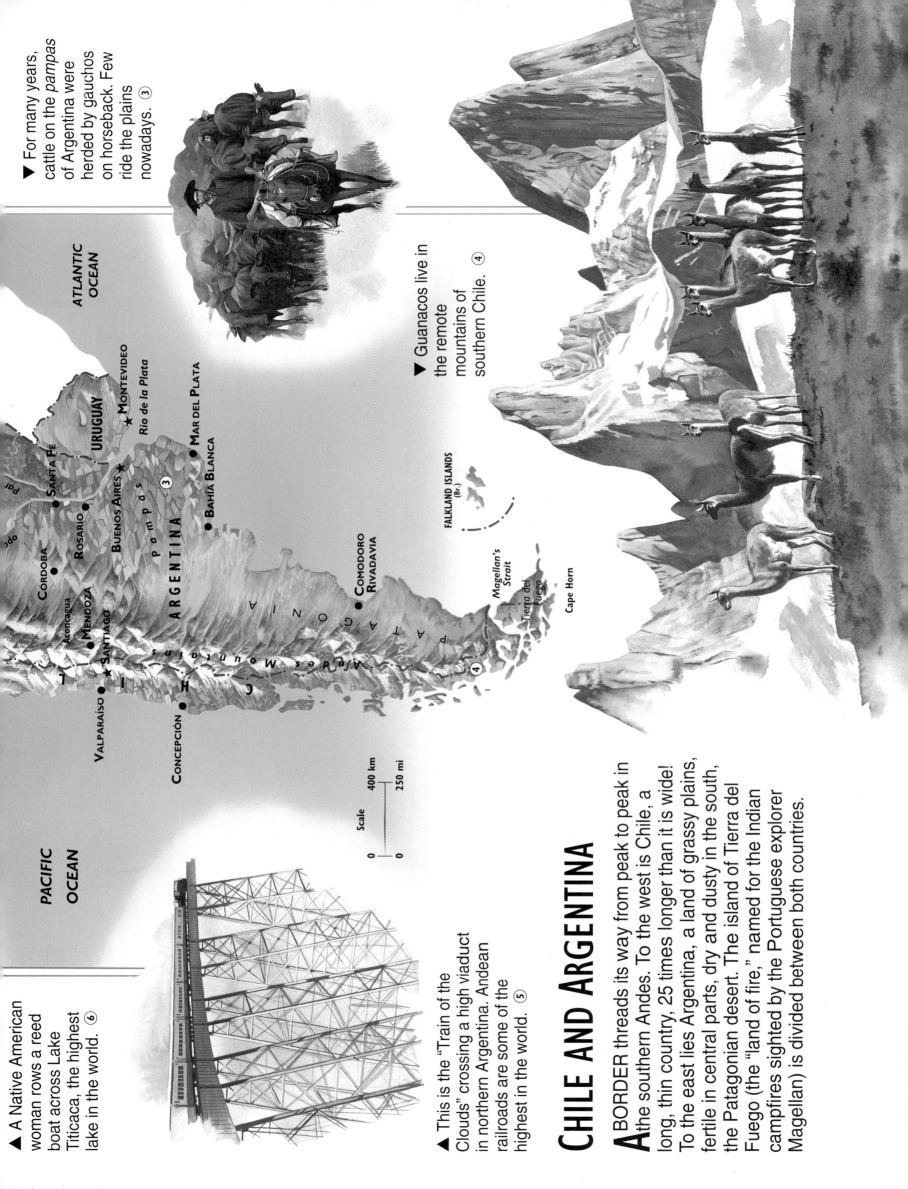

▶ For many years, cattle on the *pampas* of Argentina were herded by gauchos on horseback. Few ride the plains nowadays. ③

ATLANTIC OCEAN

▶ Guanacos live in the remote mountains of southern Chile. ④

URUGUAY
MONTEVIDEO ★
Rio de la Plata
SANTA FÉ ●
● CÓRDOBA
ROSARIO ●
BUENOS AIRES ★
③
P a m p a s
MAR DEL PLATA ●
BAHÍA BLANCA ●
Par
do
ARGENTINA
Aconcagua
MENDOZA ●
● SANTIAGO ★
Andes Mountains
C H I L E
VALPARAISO ●
CONCEPCIÓN ●
P A T A G O N I A
COMODORO RIVADAVIA ●
④
FALKLAND ISLANDS (Br.)
Magellan's Strait
Tierra del Fuego
Cape Horn

PACIFIC OCEAN

▲ A Native American woman rows a reed boat across Lake Titicaca, the highest lake in the world. ⑥

Scale
0
0
400 km
250 mi

▲ This is the "Train of the Clouds" crossing a high viaduct in northern Argentina. Andean railroads are some of the highest in the world. ⑤

CHILE AND ARGENTINA

A BORDER threads its way from peak to peak in the southern Andes. To the west is Chile, a long, thin country, 25 times longer than it is wide! To the east lies Argentina, a land of grassy plains, fertile in central parts, dry and dusty in the south, the Patagonian desert. The island of Tierra del Fuego (the "land of fire," named for the Indian campfires sighted by the Portuguese explorer Magellan) is divided between both countries.

UNITED KINGDOM

ICELAND

NORWAY

SWEDEN

FINLAND

DENMARK

POLAND

GERMANY

AUSTRIA

IRELAND

NETHERLANDS

BELGIUM

LUXEMBOURG

FRANCE

SWITZERLAND

MONACO

ITALY

VATICAN CITY

SAN MARINO

MALTA

ANDORRA

PORTUGAL

EUROPE

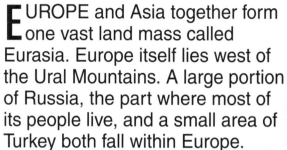

EUROPE and Asia together form one vast land mass called Eurasia. Europe itself lies west of the Ural Mountains. A large portion of Russia, the part where most of its people live, and a small area of Turkey both fall within Europe.

Europe is a land of peninsulas and islands. Their shores are lapped by the waters of the North Atlantic Ocean and its seas. Apart from the mountain ranges and the frozen Arctic lands, nearly every corner of the continent has been shaped by humans. Farmland competes for space with towns and cities, roads, airports, quarries or factories. Europe is densely populated, particularly in the lowlands of the western countries.

ICELAND

Fishing

Bearded seal

FAEROE IS.
(Denmark)

Killer whale

Fishing

Oil

Skiing

Whisky distillery

NORTH SEA

Hogs

Hogs

Sheep

IRELAND

UNITED KINGDOM

DENMARK

Fishing

Cattle

Coal

Gas

NETHERLANDS

Kiel Ca

Cattle

Channel Tunnel

BELGIUM

Industry

LUXEMBOURG

GERMANY

Cattle

Sugar beet

Beer

Grapes

Wheat

Skiing

FRANCE

SWITZERLAND

Tobacco

ATLANTIC OCEAN

Hogs

Fishing

Sheep

Grapes

Car factory

Wheat

ANDORRA

Grape harvest

Grapes

SPAIN

Tourism

Sheep

GIBRALTAR (Br.)

Oranges

MEDITERRANEAN SEA

Lemons

Tourism

SPAIN

LIECHTENSTEIN

HUNGARY

BULGARIA

ALBANIA

GREECE

SLOVENIA

CROATIA

MACEDONIA

CZECH REPUBLIC

SLOVAKIA

FACTS ABOUT EUROPE

Area 3,750,000 sq mi
Population 695,000,000
Highest point Elbrus (Russia) 18,480 ft
Lowest point Caspian Sea (Russia) 92 ft below sea level
Longest river Volga (Russia) 2,290 mi
Largest lake Ladoga (Russia) 6,835 sq mi
Largest country (excluding Russia) Ukraine 233,090 sq mi
Largest population (excluding Russia) Germany 79,753,000
Largest city Moscow (Russia) 8,769,000

Mining

Lapp herdsman

White Sea

Mining

Moose

Lumber

FINLAND

L. Ladoga

Lumber

SWEDEN

Lumber

Mechanical log cutter

Brown bear

Mining

Aircraft factory

ESTONIA

Wolf

R U S S I A

Oil

LATVIA

Potatoes

Cattle

Wheat

Volga

BALTIC SEA

Cattle

LITHUANIA

BELARUS

Flax

Corn

Sugar beet

RUSSIA

Potatoes

Hogs

Potatoes

Chernobyl Nuclear power station

ESTONIA

POLAND

Horse-drawn plow

U K R A I N E

Coal

LATVIA

Wheat

Coal

Herding cattle

Tobacco

Caspian Sea

LITHUANIA

ECH REPUBLIC

Harvesting wheat

SLOVAKIA

MOLDOVA

Mining

BELARUS

Grapes

Gas

Sheep

AUSTRIA

HUNGARY

Hogs

Elbrus

UKRAINE

OVENIA

Wheat

CROATIA

ROMANIA

Ferry

BLACK SEA

MOLDOVA

BOSNIA AND HERZEGOVINA

YUGOSLAVIA

Grapes

Sheep

Grapes

ROMANIA

Grapes

BULGARIA

ITALY

Olives

MACEDONIA

T U R K E Y

Tobacco

ALBANIA

GREECE

Aegean Sea

Olives

Tourism

CYPRUS

THE EUROPEAN UNION

Twelve countries form the European Union. They are: Belgium, Netherlands, Luxembourg, Germany, France, Italy, United Kingdom, Ireland, Denmark, Spain, Portugal and Greece. Norway, Sweden, Finland, and Austria join in 1995.

BOSNIA AND HERZEGOVINA

CYPRUS

YUGOSLAVIA

NATIONS OF EUROPE

ALBANIA
Area 11,100 sq mi **Population** 3,300,000
Capital Tiranë **Language** Albanian

ANDORRA
Area 175 sq mi **Population** 55,000
Capital Andorra **Languages** Catalan,
French, Spanish

AUSTRIA
Area 32,377 sq mi **Population** 7,712,000
Capital Vienna **Language** German

BELARUS
Area 80,155 sq mi **Pop.** 10,260,000
Capital Minsk **Language** Belorussian

BELGIUM
Area 11,783 sq mi **Pop.** 10,022,000
Capital Brussels **Languages** Dutch
(Flemish), French, German

BOSNIA AND HERZEGOVINA
Area 19,741 sq mi **Population** 4,365,000
Capital Sarajevo **Language** Serbo-Croat

▲ Irish boy ⑥

BULGARIA
Area 42,823 sq mi **Population** 8,989,000
Capital Sofia **Languages** Bulgarian,
Turkish, Macedonian

CROATIA
Area 21,823 sq mi **Population** 4,700,000
Capital Zagreb **Language** Serbo-Croat

CYPRUS
Area 3,572 sq mi **Population** 527,000
Capital Nicosia **Languages** Greek,
Turkish, English

CZECH REPUBLIC
Area 30,450 sq mi **Pop.** 10,302,000
Capital Prague **Language** Czech

DENMARK
Area 16,638 sq mi **Population** 5,162,000
Capital Copenhagen **Language** Danish

ESTONIA
Area 17,413 sq mi **Population** 1,575,000
Capital Tallinn **Languages** Estonian,
Russian

FINLAND
Area 130,559 sq mi **Pop.** 5,029,000
Capital Helsinki **Languages** Finnish,
Swedish

FRANCE
Area 211,208 sq mi **Pop.** 57,049,000
Capital Paris **Language** French

GERMANY
Area 137,882 sq mi **Pop.** 79,753,000
Capitals Berlin, Bonn **Language**
German

GREECE
Area 50,949 sq mi **Pop.** 10,020,000
Capital Athens **Language** Greek

IRELAND
Area 27,137 sq mi **Pop.** 3,523,000
Capital Dublin **Languages** English,
Irish

ITALY
Area 116,324 sq mi **Pop.** 57,746,000
Capital Rome **Language** Italian

▶ Lapp boy, from Norway ①

★ **National capital**

Scale

0   600 km

0   400 mi

HUNGARY
Area 35,921 sq mi **Pop.** 10,337,000
Capital Budapest **Language**
Hungarian

ICELAND
Area 39,769 sq mi **Pop.** 260,000
Capital Reykjavik **Language**
Icelandic

▲ Gypsy girl, from Italy ⑤

LATVIA
Area 24,595 sq mi **Pop.** 2,606,000
Capital Riga **Languages** Latvian,
Russian

LIECHTENSTEIN
Area 62 sq mi **Population** 29,000
Capital Vaduz **Language** German

LITHUANIA
Area 25,174 sq mi **Pop.** 3,761,000
Capital Vilnius **Languages**
Lithuanian, Russian, Polish

LUXEMBOURG
Area 998 sq mi **Population** 390,000
Capital Luxembourg **Languages**
German, Letzeburgesch, French

MOLDOVA
Area 13,012 sq mi **Pop.** 4,361,000
Capital Kishinev **Languages**
Moldovan, Ukrainian, Russian

MONACO
Area 0.7 sq mi **Population** 30,000
Language French

▶ Lithuanian girl ②

POLAND
Area 120,728 sq mi **Population**
38,183,000 **Capital** Warsaw **Language**
Polish

PORTUGAL
Area 35,516 sq mi **Population**
10,525,000 **Capital** Lisbon **Language**
Portuguese

ROMANIA
Area 91,699 sq mi **Population**
22,761,000 **Capital** Bucharest
Languages Romanian, Hungarian,
German

RUSSIA
Area 6,592,849 sq mi **Pop.** 148,543,000
Capital Moscow **Languages** Russian, 38
other languages

SAN MARINO
Area 24 sq mi **Population** 24,000
Language Italian

SLOVAKIA
Area 18,933 sq mi **Pop.** 5,310,000
Capital Bratislava **Languages** Slovak,
Hungarian, Czech

SLOVENIA
Area 7,819 sq mi **Population** 2,020,000
Capital Ljubljana **Languages** Slovene

SPAIN
Area 194,885 sq mi **Population** 39,322
Capital Madrid **Languages** Spanish,
Catalan, Basque, Galician

SWEDEN
Area 173,732 sq mi **Pop.** 8,644,000
Capital Stockholm **Languages** Swedish,
Finnish, Lappish

▲ Ukrainian girl ③

SWITZERLAND
Area 15,943 sq mi **Population** 6,751,000
Capital Bern **Languages** German,
French, Italian

UKRAINE
Area 233,090 sq mi **Pop.** 51,944,000
Capital Kiev **Languages** Ukrainian,
Russian

UNITED KINGDOM
Area 94,269 sq mi **Population**
57,411,000 **Capital** London **Languages**
English, Welsh

VATICAN CITY
Area 0.2 sq mi **Population** 800
Language Italian

YUGOSLAVIA
Area 39,506 sq mi **Population** 9,950,000
Capital Belgrade **Languages**
Serbo-Croat, Albanian, Hungarian

MACEDONIA
Area 9,928 sq mi **Pop.** 2,179,000
Capital Skopje **Languages**
Macedonian, Albanian

MALTA
Area 122 sq mi **Population** 360,000
Capital Valletta **Languages** Maltese,
English, Italian

NETHERLANDS
Area 16,164 sq mi **Pop.** 15,065,000
Capitals Amsterdam, The Hague
Language Dutch

NORWAY
Area 149,412 sq mi **Pop.** 4,250,000
Capital Oslo **Language** Norwegian

▲ Slovak boy ④

NORTHERN EUROPE

NORWAY, Sweden and Denmark are often grouped under the name Scandinavia. Taken together with Finland and Iceland, these are the Nordic countries of Europe.

The far north is sometimes known as the "Land of the Midnight Sun." During the summer months, the sun never goes down, the snows melt, and the Lapps graze their reindeer on the grasslands. In winter, the sun never rises. The soil freezes over and the reindeer return to the forests.

Iceland, on the edge of the Arctic Ocean, is almost treeless, a bleak landscape of volcanoes, rock and ice caps.

▲ A view of Stockholm, capital city of Sweden. ①

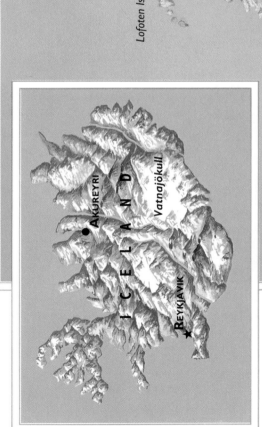

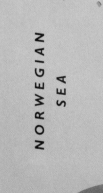

▲ Reindeer grazing in Lapland's summer pastures. ②

▲ A glassblower makes glasses in Sweden. ③

HAMMERFEST

② Inari

TROMSØ

NARVIK

KIRUNA

Lofoten Is.

OULU

LULEÅ

UMEÅ

VAASA

KUOPIO

FINLAND

LAPLAND

ÖSTERSUND

TRONDHEIM

NORWEGIAN SEA

ICELAND

AKUREYRI

Vatnajökull

REYKJAVIK

⑤

Scale

0   150 km

0   100 mi

▲ More than 1,000 years ago, the Vikings traveled out from Scandinavia in search of new lands. They sailed as far as North America. This carving shows us what a Viking warrior looked like. ④

▶ Legoland in Denmark is an amazing exhibition of sculptures and buildings, all made of plastic bricks. ⑥

HELSINKI
LAHTI
Gulf of Finland
TURKU
TALLINN
L. Peipus
ESTONIA
RIGA
LATVIA
Saaremaa
LIEPAJA
LITHUANIA
KAUNAS
VILNIUS
Åland Is.
UPPSALA ④ ①
STOCKHOLM
Gotland
VISBY
Öland
BALTIC SEA
NORRKÖPING
KARLSKRONA
Vättern
③
KARLSTAD
Vänern
GÖTEBORG
COPENHAGEN
OSLO
MALMÖ
Bornholm
Skagerrak
ÅLBORG
ÅRHUS
DENMARK
⑥
ODENSE
KRISTIANSAND
STAVANGER
BERGEN
N
O

▶ Down the west coast of Norway, long fingers of the sea reach deep inland. These are called *fjords*. On either side, mountain slopes rise steeply out of the water.

Tens of thousands of years ago, Scandinavia lay under a vast sheet of ice. Rivers of ice, called glaciers, carved deep valleys in the mountains. When the glaciers melted, the sea flooded in. The valleys became fjords.

Norway's coastline is so jagged that, if it were straightened out, it would reach halfway round the world! ⑤

BRITISH ISLES

THE BRITISH ISLES is the name given to the group of islands that lie off the northwestern coast of Europe. The two largest islands are Great Britain ("Little Britain" is Brittany in France), and Ireland. The United Kingdom consists of Great Britain, which includes England, Scotland and Wales, and Northern Ireland. The north

and west are mostly highland. Central and southern Britain are more low-lying, a mixture of rolling farmland and sprawling cities.

The sea has played an important part in Britain's history. Sailors traveled to distant parts of the globe and Britain built up one of the largest empires the world has ever seen.

▲ The Iron Bridge in Coalbrookdale, England, was the world's first bridge made of iron. ①

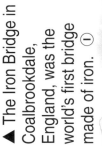

▲ Lakes and sea inlets in Scotland are known as lochs. ②

▼ Cricket, a summer sport in England. ③

▲ Little Moreton Hall was built using richly-carved wood. ⑧

▲ This part of the Northern Irish coast is called the Giant's Causeway. ⑦

Shetland Is.

Orkney Is.

NORTH SEA

Cape Wrath

INVERNESS
Loch Ness

ABERDEEN

DUNDEE

SCOTLAND

EDINBURGH

GLASGOW

CARLISLE

NEWCASTLE

MIDDLESBROUGH

②

Outer Hebrides

Skye

Mull

Islay

ATLANTIC OCEAN

Isle of Man

⑦

LONDONDERRY

NORTHERN IRELAND

Lough Neagh

BELFAST

▲ Inside this clock tower, next to the Houses of Parliament in London, is the bell known as Big Ben. It is famous for its chimes. ④

▼ All over Great Britain and Ireland, there are ruins of ancient castles. Some have massive stone walls and towers. They were built in the Middle Ages to defend a lord, his family, his servants, and his army. Edward I, who reigned from 1272 to 1307, was one of the greatest castle-builders. He built the castle in this picture at Caernarfon in Wales. It was protected on all sides by the sea, a river, and a moat. Edward I's son, who was born in Caernarfon, was the first Prince of Wales. ⑤

▲ Breeding and racing horses is popular in Ireland. Thanks to a rainy climate, the "Emerald Isle" has large areas of lush, green pasture. Most farms are devoted to raising sheep and dairy cattle, especially in the central lowlands. ⑥

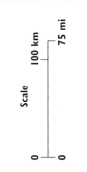

FRANCE

FRANCE is the largest country in western Europe. Wet weather sweeping in from the Atlantic is good for the pastures and orchards of Brittany and Normandy in the northwest. Eastern France can be hot in summer but very cold in winter. The south is warm enough all year round for grapes, tobacco and olive trees to grow.

▲ This train is known as the TGV, short for *Train à Grande Vitesse* (high-speed train). It is the fastest train in the world, holding the speed record of 320 mph. Since it first ran in 1981, new, straight tracks have been built for it all over France. Every journey is controlled by computers. ⑦

▲ The abbey of Mont-St-Michel stands on an old hill just off the coast of Normandy. You can go there by road, but at high tide Mont-St-Michel is completely surrounded by the sea! ⑥

◄ This man is hunting for truffles, a kind of mushroom. The best way to find them is to use a hog to sniff them out! ①

CALAIS

AMIENS

LE HAVRE

ROUEN

NORMANDY

PARIS

BREST

⑥

BRITTANY

RENNES

⑦

LE MANS

ORLÉANS

TOURS

Loire

Cher

NANTES

POITIERS

Vienne

LA ROCHELLE

BAY OF BISCAY

LIMOGES

①

BORDEAUX

Dordogne ②

Lot

Tarn

Scale

0   100 km

0   75 mi

GASCONY

⑤

BIARRITZ

TOULOUSE

Garonne

Pyrenees

◀ The cave paintings at Lascaux were discovered (accidentally) by four boys in 1940. ②

◀ The Eiffel Tower was built for the Paris exhibition in 1889. It was then the tallest building in the world. Standing 990 feet, it was nearly twice the height of the next tallest, the Washington Monument. In hot weather, it grows by another seven inches as the metal expands. It took 230 men just over two years to build the tower – quick work in those days. The 18,000 pieces of iron were hammered together using 2.5 million rivets.

At first, many people thought the Eiffel Tower ugly and unsafe. Now it is one of the best-known landmarks in the world. ③

LILLE

RDY

Oise

REIMS

Marne

METZ

NANCY

Seine

STRASBOURG

CHAMPAGNE

Vosges

MULHOUSE

DIJON

BURGUNDY

Saône

Allier

Loire

CLERMONT-FERRAND

LYON

ssif

Isère

tral

ALPS

GRENOBLE

Rhône

▲ France was once part of the Roman empire. The Romans constructed many magnificent roads and buildings. Still standing today is this aqueduct, called the Pont du Gard. It was built outside Nîmes nearly 2,000 years ago. It used to carry water into the city from nearby hills. ④

AVIGNON

④

NÎMES

NICE

MONACO

MONTPELLIER

PROVENCE

MARSEILLE

TOULON

MEDITERRANEAN SEA

PERPIGNAN

CORSICA

AJACCIO

◀ Many French people enjoy riding bicycles. The *Tour de France* is the world's greatest bicycle race. For three weeks in July, hundreds of riders speed through the French countryside (and often through neighboring countries as well). ⑤

THE NETHERLANDS

NEARLY ALL of the Netherlands is completely flat. One third of the land actually lies below the level of the sea! Sand dunes, earth embankments called dikes, and sea walls keep the sea water from flooding in.

Many areas once actually lay underwater. People dug ditches and built windmills to pump the water away along canals. In this way, they *reclaimed* the land from the sea. These polderlands, as they are called, are used for farmland and pasture.

The Netherlands are sometimes known as Holland, although this name really refers only to one part of the country. It is one of the most densely populated nations in the world.

▲ The Dutch countryside is criss-crossed by canals and dotted with windmills. ①

▲ The Skinny Bridge in Amsterdam. ②

▶ Carrying cheeses to market in Alkmaar. ③

▲ Rotterdam, located near the mouth of the Rhine River, is the busiest port in the world. ⑧

GRONINGEN

ENSCHEDE

ZWOLLE

APELDOORN

ARNHEM

NIJMEGEN

LEEUWARDEN

Maas

IJsselmeer

Wadden Sea

Frisian Islands

N E T H E R L A N D S

UTRECHT

Lek

Waal

EINDHOVEN

AMSTERDAM ②

TILBURG

DEN HELDER

ALKMAAR ③

HAARLEM

LEIDEN

DORDRECHT ①

ROTTERDAM ⑧

BREDA

THE HAGUE

Rhine-Maas Delta

NORTH SEA

BELGIUM AND LUXEMBOURG

NORTHERN BELGIUM is quite like its neighbor, the Netherlands. It is mostly flat farmland laced with canals and cities. The people speak Dutch, or Flemish as they call it. South of Brussels, the capital, rolling hills start to appear. Beyond the River Meuse lie the wooded hills and valleys of the Ardennes hills. This is the home of the French-speaking people known as Walloons.

Farther south lies the Grand Duchy of Luxembourg. Most Luxembourgers speak German, or their version of it called Letzeburgesch.

▲ The castle of Vianden in the wooded hills of Luxembourg. ④

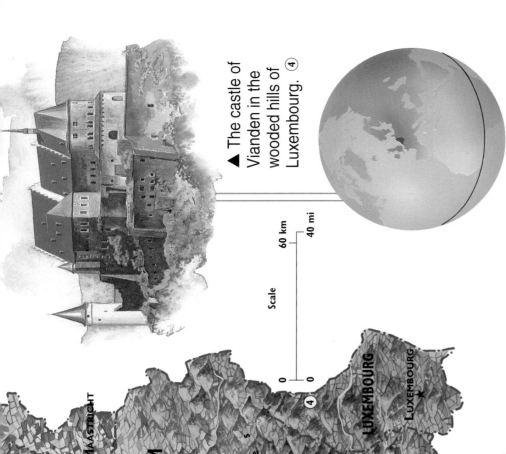

▲ This fishing vessel is setting out from a Dutch port for the rich fishing grounds of the North Sea. ⑦

▲ The Atomium is a museum of science in Brussels. ⑥

▶ Bruges, like nearby Ghent, grew rich in the Middle Ages from the wool and cloth industry in Flanders. ⑤

Scale

60 km

40 mi

0

0

OOSTENDE ⑤

F L A N D E R S

GHENT

Scheldt

BRUSSELS ⑥★

MAASTRICHT

LIÈGE

B E L G I U M

Meuse

NAMUR

MONS

CHARLEROI

Sambre

W A L L O N I A

A r d e n n e s

LUXEMBOURG

LUXEMBOURG ★

④

PORTUGAL

NOWHERE in Portugal is very far from the sea. More than 500 years ago, men from Portugal set off to cross the oceans and explore the continents of Africa and Asia. Today, sea fishing is an important industry. Portugal is also famous for its cork trees and a sweet wine, called port, made from local grapes.

◀ This is an old Portuguese fishing boat, called a *moliceiro*. ①

▶ An old woman from a small village in southern Portugal. ②

▲ This is the Dom Luis Bridge. It crosses the Douro River as it flows through the city of Porto, Portugal's second largest city. Cars can drive on upper or lower roadways. ⑥

▶ These windmills stand on the plains of La Mancha in central Spain. In a famous Spanish tale, an old knight called Don Quixote mistakes the windmills for giants. He even rode his horse into battle with them! ⑤

► Spanish kings lived at El Escorial 400 years ago. They ruled over much of Europe and America. ③

SPAIN

ONLY A FEW MILES of sea lies between Spain and northwest Africa. In the far south, the climate is almost the same: very hot and dry in summer. The north of the country is wetter and greener. Not all the people here speak Spanish. The Basques, Galicians, and Catalans have their own languages.

SAN SEBASTIÁN

BASQUE PROVINCES

Pyrenees

ANDORRA

A R A G O N

ZARAGOZA

Ebro

LÉRIDA

C A T A L O N I A

BARCELONA

N

CUENCA

Scale

0   100 km

0   75 mi

Menorca

Mallorca

PALMA

VALENCIA

Júcar

ancha

ALBACETE

Ibiza

ALICANTE

MURCIA

MEDITERRANEAN SEA

CARTAGENA

▲ Arab people from Africa, called the Moors, once ruled Spain. They were driven out of Spain more than 500 years ago. They left behind them great palaces, castles, and mosques (their places of worship). The Alhambra was a Moorish palace built on a hill in the city of Granada. This picture shows the Court of Lions in the Alhambra. It was named for the carved lion statues around the fountain. ④

GERMANY

FLAT northern Germany is part of the North European Plain. Travel east and the first uplands you come to are the Urals in Russia. Go south, through Germany, and you will soon find a landscape of wooded hills and fertile valleys. Eventually, at the Austrian border, you will reach the towering peaks of the Alps.

Germany became a single country for the first time in 1871. Before then, Germans lived in a jigsaw land of duchies, principalities, and kingdoms. It was divided into East and West after World War Two in 1945, but became one country again in 1990.

▲ For nearly 30 years, Berlin was divided by a wall. Now people can once again walk through the Brandenburg Gate. ①

▲ River boats and barges steer through the Rhine gorge. The hillsides are covered with vines and topped by ancient castles. ②

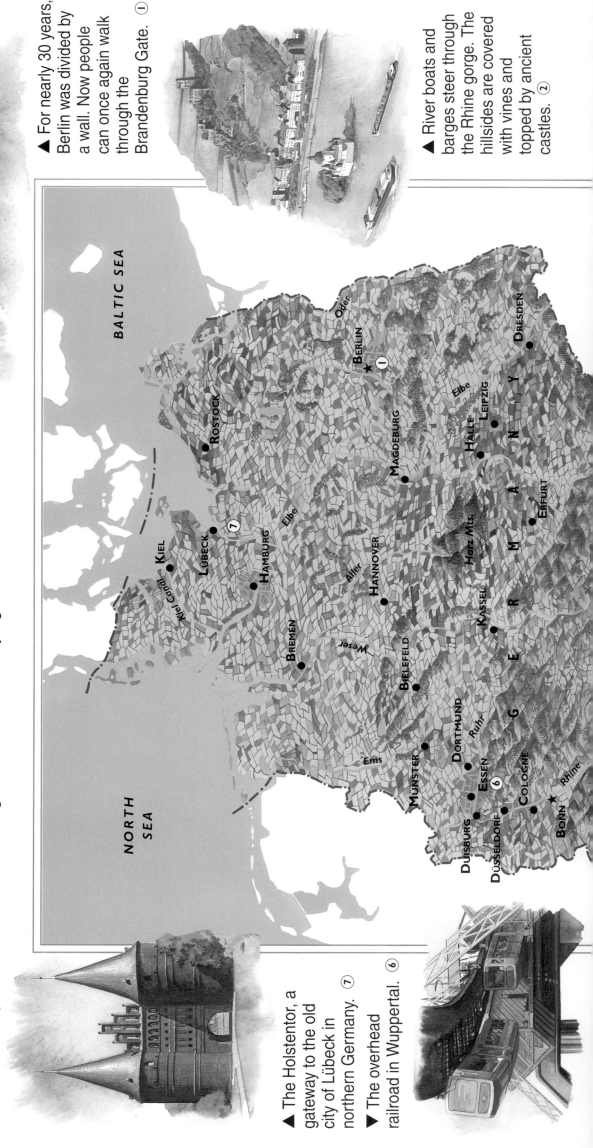

▲ The Holstentor, a gateway to the old city of Lübeck in northern Germany. ⑦

▶ The overhead railroad in Wuppertal. ⑥

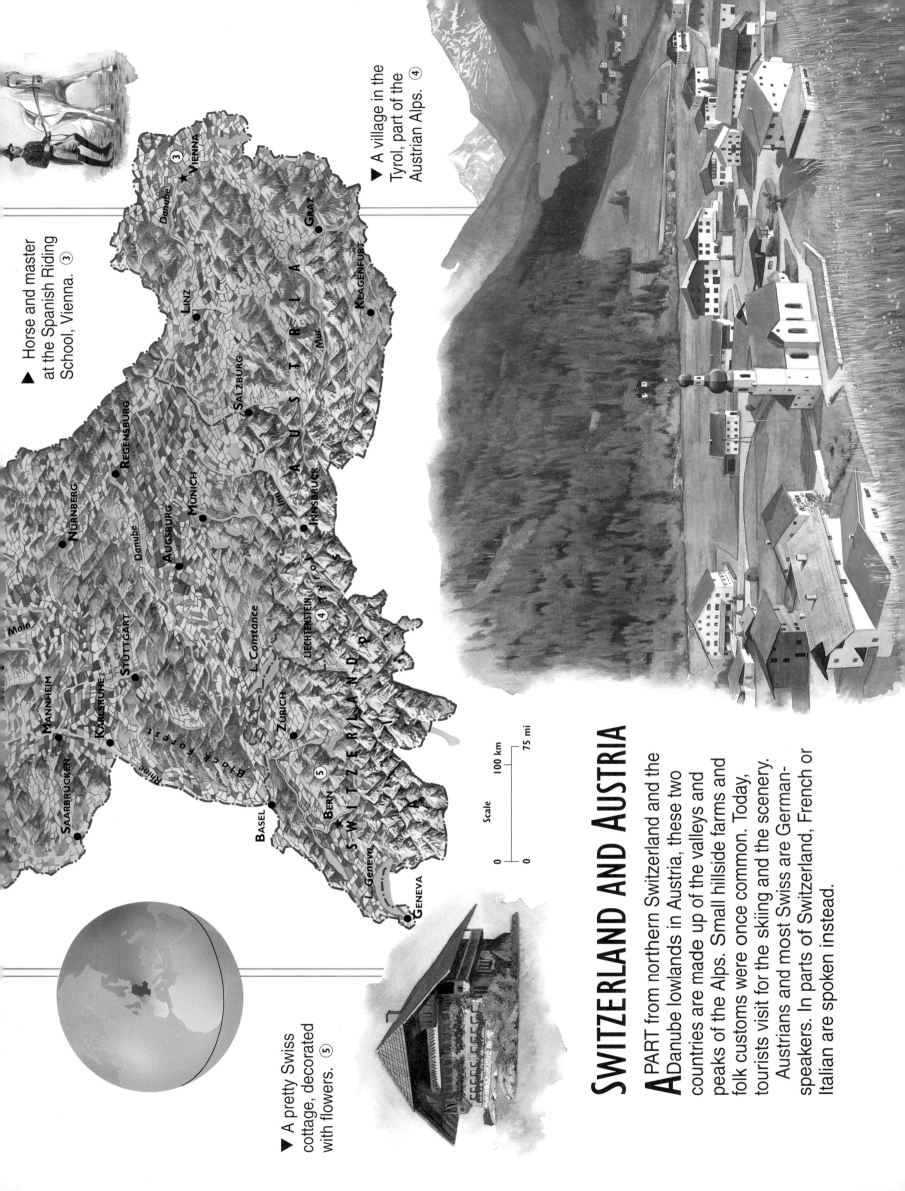

▲ Horse and master at the Spanish Riding School, Vienna. ③

▶ A village in the Tyrol, part of the Austrian Alps. ④

NÜRNBERG

REGENSBURG

Danube

AUGSBURG

MUNICH

MANNHEIM

STUTTGART

KARLSRUHE

SAARBRÜCKEN

Main

Black Forest

Rhine

L. Constance

ZÜRICH

LIECHTENSTEIN ④

INNSBRUCK

T y r o l

I n n

S

SALZBURG

LINZ

Danube

VIENNA ③

GRAZ

Mur

KLAGENFURT

A U S T R I A

S W I T Z E R L A N D

A l p s

BASEL

BERN ⑤

L. Geneva

GENEVA

Scale

0 ——— 100 km

0 ——— 75 mi

▶ A pretty Swiss cottage, decorated with flowers. ⑤

SWITZERLAND AND AUSTRIA

APART from northern Switzerland and the Danube lowlands in Austria, these two countries are made up of the valleys and peaks of the Alps. Small hillside farms and folk customs were once common. Today, tourists visit for the skiing and the scenery. Austrians and most Swiss are German-speakers. In parts of Switzerland, French or Italian are spoken instead.

ITALY

POINTING out into the Mediterranean Sea, Italy is shaped like a boot. It looks as if it is about to kick the island of Sicily! All around Italy's northern borders are the Alps. These high, craggy mountains separate the country from the rest of Europe. Lower mountains, called the Apennines, run the length of the boot, all the way down to the "toe" in the south.

Away from the high ground, Italy has a warm climate. Grape vines, olives, and fruit trees grow all over the country. In the flat, fertile plain of the Po River, farmers grow a special type of wheat, called durum. It is used to make pasta.

▲ Venice is built on an island in a lagoon, a shallow bay. Canals are its streets, and gondolas, like this one, are its cabs. ①

▲ A range of jagged peaks in the Alps in northeastern Italy is known as the Dolomites. ②

▲ Wolves, bears, and wild boar still roam the hills of central Italy. ⑧

▲ Soccer is a very popular sport in Italy. Huge crowds watch the big matches. ⑦

Scale
0 ——— 100 km
0 ——— 75 mi

ADRIATIC SEA

TRIESTE

BOLZANO ②

BRESCIA

MILAN ⑦

TURIN

GENOA

Po

Adda

Adige

VERONA

PADOVA

VENICE ①

Po

PARMA

LA SPEZIA

BOLOGNA

SAN MARINO

ANCONA

PESCARA

FLORENCE

Arno

Livorno

Elba

PERUGIA

⑤

TERNI

Tiber

VATICAN CITY ★ ROME ③

⑧

42

▲ A cardinal, a senior Roman Catholic churchman from Vatican City State. ③

▼ These are the remains of Pompeii, a Roman town covered in ash when the volcano Vesuvius erupted in 79 A.D. ④

▼ San Gimignano is a small town in Tuscany, central Italy. It is famous for its towers. Only 15 remain out of the 72 built more than 600 years ago (some towers cannot be seen in this picture).

Hundreds of years ago, Italy was not a single country at all, but made up of a large number of tiny states. San Gimignano was one of these states. ⑤

▲ Known as *trulli*, these peculiar houses in the southern town of Alberobello are shaped like pepperpots. Their roofs are built from stone slabs. ⑥

BARI
⑥ BRINDISI
TARANTO

Vesuvius
SALERNO
④
NAPLES

REGGIO DI CALABRIA
MESSINA
Etna
CATANIA
Stromboli

PALERMO
S I C I L Y

T Y R R H E N I A N   S E A

M E D I T E R R A N E A N   S E A

MALTA
★ VALLETTA

Pantelleria

SASSARI
S A R D I N I A
CAGLIARI

EASTERN EUROPE

CROSS THE ODER River into Poland from Germany and you enter eastern Europe. The North European Plain fans out to meet the shores of the Black Sea in the south. In between the industrial cities, nearly all the countryside is farmland. Ukraine, with its "black earth," has the most fertile land.

◀ All over eastern Europe, people live and work on small farms. Animals like chickens, hogs, and these geese are valuable possessions. ①

▲ In eastern Europe, traditional costumes are worn for important occasions. This is a couple at a wedding in Slovakia. ⑦

▼ Prague castle stands on a hill overlooking the Czech capital city. Inside its walls, you will find a cathedral, palaces, narrow, winding streets, and squares. St. Vaclav, "Good King Wenceslas," is buried here. ⑥

BALTIC SEA

KALININGRAD

PART OF RUSSIA

GDANSK

SZCZECIN

BIALYSTOK

Vistula

Bug

POZNAN

WARSAW

BREST

Pripet Marsh

P O L A N D

LODZ

Oder

WROCLAW

PRAGUE ⑥

④

KRAKOW

CZECH REPUBLIC

KATOWICE

②

BRNO

Carpathian Mts.

Dniester

LVOV

S L O V A K I A

KOSICE

⑦

BRATISLAVA

BUDAPEST

①

DEBRECEN

H U N G A R Y

L. Balaton

Danube

SZEGED

PÉCS

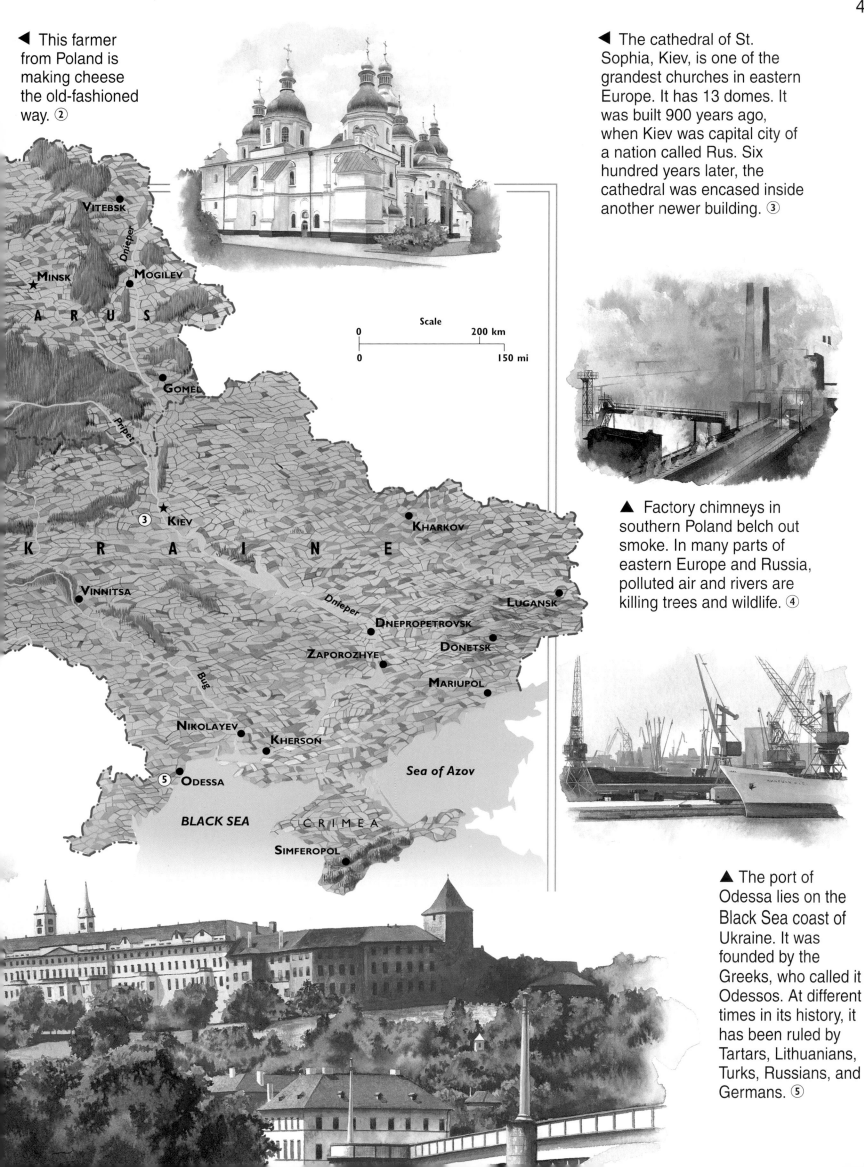

◀ This farmer from Poland is making cheese the old-fashioned way. ②

◀ The cathedral of St. Sophia, Kiev, is one of the grandest churches in eastern Europe. It has 13 domes. It was built 900 years ago, when Kiev was capital city of a nation called Rus. Six hundred years later, the cathedral was encased inside another newer building. ③

▲ Factory chimneys in southern Poland belch out smoke. In many parts of eastern Europe and Russia, polluted air and rivers are killing trees and wildlife. ④

▲ The port of Odessa lies on the Black Sea coast of Ukraine. It was founded by the Greeks, who called it Odessos. At different times in its history, it has been ruled by Tartars, Lithuanians, Turks, Russians, and Germans. ⑤

VITEBSK

Dnieper

MINSK

MOGILEV

A R U S

GOMEL

Pripet

Scale

0   200 km

0   150 mi

③ KIEV

KHARKOV

K R A I N E

VINNITSA

Dnieper

LUGANSK

DNEPROPETROVSK

ZAPOROZHYE

DONETSK

Bug

MARIUPOL

NIKOLAYEV

KHERSON

Sea of Azov

⑤ ODESSA

BLACK SEA

C R I M E A

SIMFEROPOL

THE BALKANS

THE SOUTHEASTERN corner of Europe is called the Balkans. The best farmland lies close to the Danube River in Serbia, Romania, and Bulgaria. The broad valley of the Danube narrows to a small gap between the steep slopes of the Iron Gate gorge.

The Balkans are a dense patchwork of different peoples and small nations. It may be years before they all live together in peace.

▲ The Corinth Canal was cut through a narrow strip of land in Greece 100 years ago. Seagoing vessels are towed through by tugboats. ⑦

► This is the Acropolis, a city of temples 2,500 years old. It was built on a hill overlooking Athens, now capital city of Greece. The most famous temple is the Parthenon, at right. If you stood on the temple steps in the days of ancient Greece, you could look out for enemy ships approaching the coast. ⑥

◄ This is a farm building in Slovenia. Called a *kozolec*, it is used for drying and storing hay. ①

◄ A Romanian shepherd in traditional costume from the Carpathian Mountains. ②

◄ Alexander Nevski Cathedral is located in Bulgaria's capital city, Sofia. It was completed less than 100 years ago, soon after Bulgaria freed itself from Turkish rule. Alexander Nevski was a Russian prince who lived in the Middle Ages. He was deeply admired by all Slavs for his victories in battle. ③

▲ This is a whirling dervish, a Muslim worshipper from Konya in Turkey who performs a wild dance. ④

▼ People still live in these ancient cave-houses in Cappadocia, Turkey. ⑤

BLACK SEA

SAMSUN

ANKARA ★

ERZURUM

T U R K E Y

Kizilirmak

L. Van

ESKIŞEHIR

⑤

KAYSERI

DIYARBAKIR

Tigris

L. Tuz

Euphrates

④ KONYA

GAZIANTEP

ADANA

ANTALYA

Scale

0   200 km

0   150 mi

CYPRUS

NICOSIA ★

TURKEY

MOST of the lands on this map (and on page 54) were once under Turkish rule. A small part of Europe around Istanbul still belongs to Turkey. Most of the country lies across the Bosporus strait in Asia. About half of all Turks still work in the fields, many on small hill farms with just a few sheep and goats.

RUSSIA
KAZAKHSTAN
TURKMENISTAN
UZBEKISTAN
TAJIKISTAN
KYRGYZSTAN
MONGOLIA
CHINA
NORTH KOREA

ARMENIA
GEORGIA
AZERBAIJAN
TURKEY
SYRIA
LEBANON
ISRAEL
JORDAN
SAUDI ARABIA
YEMEN

ARCTIC OCEAN

Mining

Ural Mts

Industry

Wolf

Gas

Mining

RUSSIA

Lynx

Potatoes

Industry

Oil

Coal

Lynx

EUROPE

Mining

Rye

Bosporus

Goat

Rye

Camel

KAZAKHSTAN

MEDITERRANEAN SEA

TURKEY

GEORGIA

Caspian Sea

Tea

Gazelle

Horseman

ARMENIA

AZERBAIJAN

UZBEKISTAN

KYRGYZSTAN

Fruit

LEBANON

SYRIA

Cotton gathering

Cotton

Oil

ISRAEL

Dead Sea

IRAQ

Dates

TURKMENISTAN

TAJIKISTAN

Camel

JORDAN

IRAN

Goat

AFGHANISTAN

TIBET

Camel

KUWAIT

Oil

Leopard

PAKISTAN

Butter churning

Yak

BAHRAIN

Oil

Sugar cane

NEPAL

Mt. Everest

BHUTAN

QATAR

RED SEA

SAUDI ARABIA

UNITED ARAB EMIRATES

BANGLA-DESH

AFRICA

Dates

Cattle

Camel

OMAN

Dates

INDIA

MYANMAR (BURMA)

YEMEN

Oryx

Rice

Millet

Dhow

Tobacco

Fishing

ARABIAN SEA

BAY OF BENGAL

Cashew nuts

SRI LANKA

Tea

MALDIVES

Fishing

Equator

INDIAN OCEAN

FACTS ABOUT ASIA

Area 16,988,000 sq mi
Population 3,337,800,000
Highest point Mt. Everest (Nepal and China) 29,028 ft
Lowest point Dead Sea (Israel and Jordan) 1,339 ft below sea level
Longest river Yangtse (China) 3,436 mi
Largest lake Caspian Sea 143,000 sq mi
Largest country Russia (including European part) 6,592,849 sq mi
Largest population China 1,200,000,000
Largest city Seoul (South Korea) 10,522,000

OMAN
UNITED ARAB EMIRATES
QATAR
BAHRAIN

SOUTH KOREA

JAPAN

TAIWAN

PHILIPPINES

INDONESIA

MALAYSIA

SINGAPORE

VIETNAM

CAMBODIA

LAOS

THAILAND

MYANMAR (BURMA)

BANGLADESH

BHUTAN

NEPAL

INDIA

SRI LANKA

MALDIVES

PAKISTAN

AFGHANISTAN

IRAN

ASIA

REACHING NEARLY halfway around the globe, Asia is the largest continent of all. The Ural and Caucasus Mountains mark the boundaries with Europe to the west. Russia, the world's largest country, lies partly in Asia and partly in Europe.

Coniferous forest, frozen plains, high mountains, and rocky desert cover vast areas of Asia. Few people live in these parts. By contrast, more than half the world's population of 5 billion people is crowded into south and east Asia. This is rich farming country. Forests are cleared to make even more room for fields. Many kinds of animals that once lived there have now become endangered.

Caribou
Lemming
Coal
SIBERIA
Seal
Brown bear
Soybeans
Rice harvesting
NGOLIA
Sheep
Coal
NORTH KOREA
Mining
SOUTH KOREA
JAPAN
Corn
Fruit
INA
Industry
Fishing
Yangtse
PACIFIC OCEAN
Hogs
TAIWAN
Tobacco
Rice
Giant panda
Fishing with cormorants
Planting rice
LAOS
LAND
Junk
PHILIPPINES
Logging
VIETNAM
Oil
CAMBODIA
Rubber
Copra
Rice
BRUNEI
MALAYSIA
Cloves
Spiny anteater
Tin mining
SINGAPORE
Orangutan
INDONESIA
Rubber
Planting rice

KUWAIT

IRAQ

RICE TERRACES

For three out of every five people in the world, rice is their main food. All over south and east Asia, rice is grown in waterlogged fields, called paddies. Where the land is hilly, wide steps, or terraces, are built into the slopes.

NATIONS OF ASIA

AFGHANISTAN
Area 251,773 sq mi **Pop.** 15,900,000
Capital Kabul **Languages** Pashto, Dari

ARMENIA
Area 11,506 sq mi **Population** 3,305,000
Capital Yerevan **Language** Armenian

AZERBAIJAN
Area 33,436 sq mi **Population** 7,021,000
Capital Baku **Language** Azeri

BAHRAIN
Area 267 sq mi **Population** 412,000
Capital Manama **Language** Arabic

BANGLADESH
Area 55,598 sq mi **Pop.** 102,563,000
Capital Dhaka **Languages** Bengali

BHUTAN
Area 18,147 sq mi **Population** 1,447,000
Capital Thimphu **Language** Dzongkha

BRUNEI
Area 2,226 sq mi **Population** 226,000
Capital Bandar Seri Begawan
Languages Malay, Chinese

▲ Indian girl ⑥

CAMBODIA
Area 69,898 sq mi **Pop.** 8,345,000
Capital Phnom Penh **Language** Khmer

CHINA
Area 3,695,500 sq mi **Population**
1,141,530,000 **Capital** Beijing **Language**
Chinese (many dialects)

GEORGIA
Area 26,911 sq mi **Population** 5,401,000
Capital Tbilisi **Language** Georgian

HONG KONG
Area 412 sq mi **Population** 5,533,000
Languages Chinese, English

INDIA
Area 1,269,350 sq mi **Pop.** 853,400,000
Capital New Delhi **Languages** Hindi,
Bengali, Bihari, Telugu, Marathi, Tamil

INDONESIA
Area 735,358 sq mi **Pop.** 189,400,000
Capital Jakarta **Language** Indonesian

IRAN
Area 636,269 sq mi **Pop.** 49,857,384
Capital Tehran **Language** Farsi

IRAQ
Area 169,235 sq mi **Pop.** 16,110,000
Capital Baghdad **Language** Arabic

ISRAEL
Area 8,473 sq mi **Pop.** 4,406,500 **Capital**
Jerusalem **Languages** Hebrew, Arabic

JAPAN
Area 145,875 sq mi **Population**
123,850,000 **Capital** Tokyo **Language**
Japanese

JORDAN
Area 37,738 sq mi **Population**
4,100,000 **Capital** Amman **Language**
Arabic

▶ Omani boy ①

LAOS
Area 91,400 sq mi **Pop.** 4,218,000
Capital Viangchan **Languages** Lao,
French

LEBANON
Area 4,036 sq mi **Population** 3,360,000
Capital Beirut **Language** Arabic

★ **National capital**

KAZAKHSTAN
Area 1,049,155 sq mi **Pop.** 16,690,300
Capital Alma-Ata **Languages** Kazakh,
Russian

KUWAIT
Area 6,880 sq mi **Pop.** 2,189,000
Capital Kuwait **Language** Arabic

KYRGYZSTAN
Area 76,640 sq mi **Population** 4,372,000
Capital Bishkek **Language** Kyrgyz

▲ Vietnamese boy ⑤

MACAO
Area 6 sq mi **Population** 462,000

MALAYSIA
Area 127,320 sq mi **Population.**
17,900,000 **Capital** Kuala Lumpur
Language Malay

MALDIVES
Area 115 sq mi **Population** 200,000
Capital Malé **Language** Divehi

MONGOLIA
Area 604,250 sq mi **Pop.** 1,900,000
Capital Ulan Bator **Language** Kalkha
Mongol

MYANMAR (BURMA)
Area 261,218 sq mi **Pop.** 46,300,000
Capital Rangoon **Language** Burmese

▶ Yakut girl,
from Russia ②

PHILIPPINES
Area 115,831 sq mi **Pop.** 62,170,000
Capital Manila **Languages** English,
Pilipino

QATAR
Area 4,416 sq mi **Population** 369,000
Capital Doha **Language** Arabic

RUSSIA
Area 6,592,849 sq mi **Pop.** 148,543,000
Capital Moscow **Languages** Russian, 38
other languages

SAUDI ARABIA
Area 926,745 sq mi **Population**
13,612,000 **Capital** Riyadh **Language**
Arabic

SINGAPORE
Area 238 sq mi **Population** 2,757,000
Languages Chinese, English, Malay,
Tamil

SOUTH KOREA
Area 38,230 sq mi **Pop.** 42,082,000
Capital Seoul **Language** Korean

SRI LANKA
Area 24,886 sq mi **Pop.** 17,200,000
Capital Colombo **Languages** Sinhalese,
Tamil, English

SYRIA
Area 71,498 sq mi **Pop.** 12,315,000
Capital Damascus **Language** Arabic

TAIWAN
Area 13,890 sq mi **Population**
20,200,000 **Capital** Taipei **Language**
Chinese

TAJIKISTAN
Area 55,250 sq mi **Pop.** 5,112,000
Capital Dushanbe **Language** Tajik

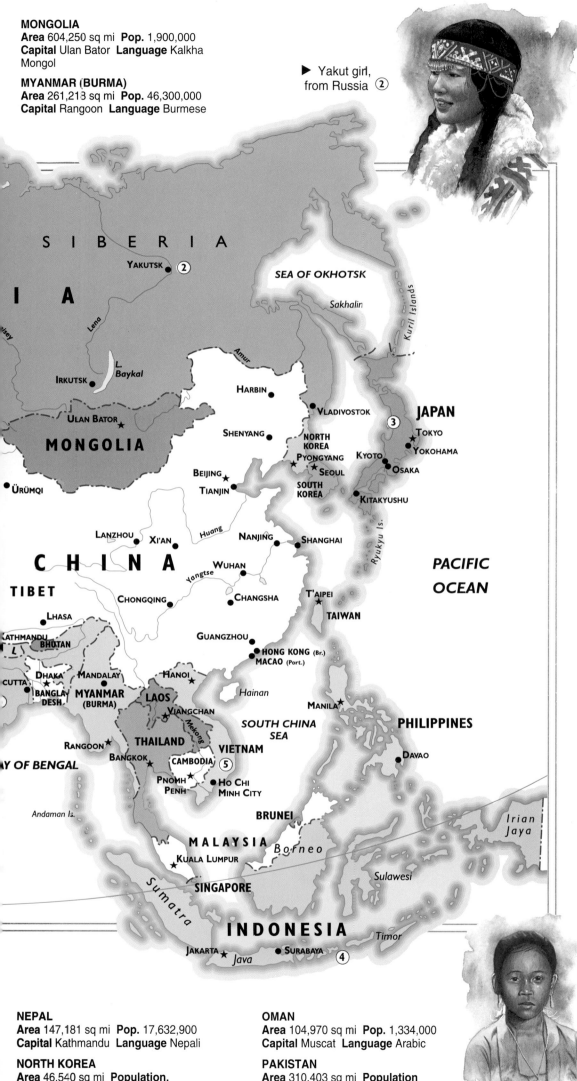

▲ Japanese boy ③

THAILAND
Area 198,115 sq mi **Pop.** 54,536,000
Capital Bangkok **Language** Thai

TURKEY
Area 300,948 sq mi **Pop.** 63,720,000
Capital Ankara **Language** Turkish

TURKMENISTAN
Area 188,455 sq mi **Pop.** 3,621,700
Capital Ashkhabad **Language** Turkmen

UNITED ARAB EMIRATES
Area 29,010 sq mi **Pop.** 11,384,000
Capital Abu Dhabi **Language** Arabic

UZBEKISTAN
Area 172,740 sq mi **Pop.** 20,322,000
Capital Tashkent **Language** Uzbek

VIETNAM
Area 127,246 sq mi **Pop.** 70,200,000
Capital Hanoi **Languages** Vietnamese,
French

YEMEN
Area 184,345 sq mi **Pop.** 11,494,000
Capital San'a **Language** Arabic

NEPAL
Area 147,181 sq mi **Pop.** 17,632,900
Capital Kathmandu **Language** Nepali

NORTH KOREA
Area 46,540 sq mi **Population.**
21,390,000 **Capital** Pyongyang
Language Korean

OMAN
Area 104,970 sq mi **Pop.** 1,334,000
Capital Muscat **Language** Arabic

PAKISTAN
Area 310,403 sq mi **Population**
114,600,000 **Capital** Islamabad
Language Urdu

▲ Balinese girl ④

RUSSIA

THE LARGEST country in the world, Russia reaches all the way from eastern Europe to within a few miles of Alaska in North America.

Most Russians live west of the Urals. Stretching away to the east are the endless forests, mountains, and bleak plains of Siberia.

◀ A carpet-maker from Tajikistan. ①

▶ Many Russian churches have spires that look like onions. This one is made entirely out of wood. ②

▲ This statue, "The Motherland," is nearly the height of the Statue of Liberty. It stands in Volgograd. During World War Two, when the city was known as Stalingrad, it was here that the Russian army defeated the German invasion force. ⑥

MURMANSK

BARENTS SEA

Novaya Zemlya

White Sea

ST. PETERSBURG

L. Ladoga

②

L. Onega

MOSCOW ⑤

Ural Mountains

R U S S

TULA

NIZHNIY NOVGOROD

VORONEZH

KAZAN

Volga

SAMARA

Ob

YEKATERINBURG

ROSTOV

⑥

VOLGOGRAD

TRANS-SIBERIAN RAILROAD

ASTRAKHAN

GEORGIA

TBILISI

Caspian Sea

OMSK

Yenisei

ARMENIA

YEREVAN

K A Z A K H S T A N

NOVOSIBIRSK

KRASNOYAR

AZERBAIJAN

Irtysh

Aral Sea

BAKU

④

Syr Darya

L. Balkhash

TURKMENISTAN

Amu Darya

ASHKHABAD

UZBEKISTAN

TASHKENT

BISHKEK

ALMA-ATA

SAMARKAND

KYRGYZSTAN

①

DUSHANBE

TAJIKISTAN

◀ A trip along the Trans-Siberian railroad is the longest rail journey you can make anywhere in the world. It takes 8 days to travel from Moscow to Vladivostok. ③

▼ The Aral Sea, one of the world's largest lakes, is gradually drying up. In the past, the Syr Darya and Amu Darya Rivers flowed into it. Their waters have been used in the cotton fields, however, and the flow has been reduced to a trickle. Now fishing boats lie stranded on the dry lake bottom. ④

CENTRAL ASIA

THE LANDS to the east of the Caspian Sea are very dry. Five new nations occupy this region. They were once part of the Soviet Union, a country made up of 15 republics, including Russia, the largest. The people who live in Central Asia are mostly Muslims.

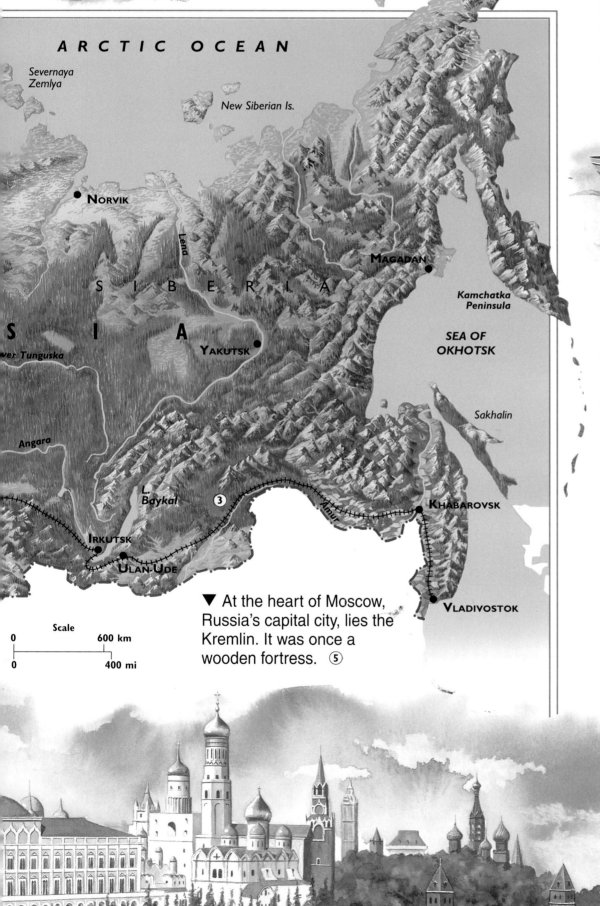

A R C T I C   O C E A N

Severnaya Zemlya

New Siberian Is.

NORVIK

Lena

S I B E R I A

S I A

ver Tunguska

YAKUTSK

MAGADAN

Kamchatka Peninsula

SEA OF OKHOTSK

Sakhalin

Angara

L. Baykal

③

Amur

KHABAROVSK

IRKUTSK

ULAN-UDE

VLADIVOSTOK

Scale

0 ——— 600 km

0 ——— 400 mi

▼ At the heart of Moscow, Russia's capital city, lies the Kremlin. It was once a wooden fortress. ⑤

THE MIDDLE EAST

THE REGION that lies between Africa and South Asia is called the Middle East. It includes the Arabian peninsula, an L-shaped land lapped on three sides by the waters of the Red Sea, the Arabian Sea, and the Persian Gulf. Nearly all of it is desert. In one place, there is mile after mile of windblown sand dunes. No one lives here at all. It is called Rub al Khali, "The Empty Quarter."

Two great rivers, the Tigris and Euphrates, flow southeast to the Persian Gulf. Between them, almost an island, lies Mesopotamia, perhaps the land of the Garden of Eden described in the Bible. It was here, thousands of years ago, that people first learned to farm.

▲ Behind this entrance is part of an ancient city. It was built into the cliffs at Petra, Jordan. The Nabateans, a desert people, lived here in ancient times. ①

▼ A street seller in Jerusalem pours a glass of tamarindy, a fruit drink. ⑤

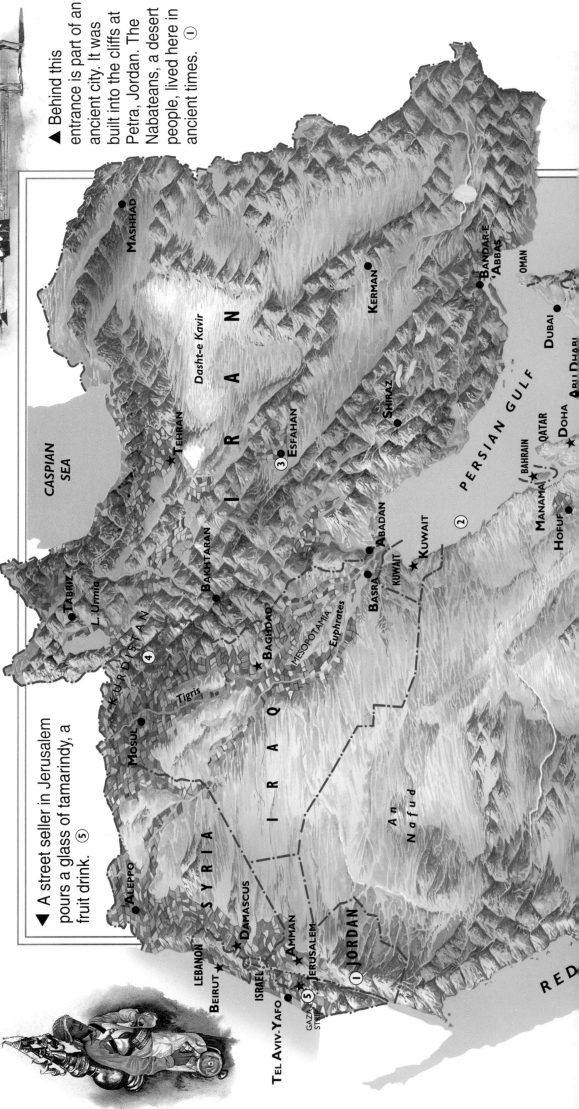

MASHHAD

BANDAR-E 'ABBAS

OMAN

KERMAN

DUBAI

ABU DHABI

Dasht-e Kavir

I R A N

SHIRAZ

PERSIAN GULF

CASPIAN SEA

TEHRAN

ESFAHAN ③

QATAR

DOHA

BAHRAIN

MANAMA

HOFUF

②

KUWAIT

KUWAIT

ABADAN

BASRA

BAKHTARAN

TABRIZ
L. Urmia

K U R D I S T A N

BAGHDAD

MESOPOTAMIA

Euphrates

④

Tigris

MOSUL

I R A Q

An Nafud

S Y R I A

ALEPPO

DAMASCUS

AMMAN

JORDAN ①

LEBANON

BEIRUT

ISRAEL

TEL AVIV-YAFO

JERUSALEM ⑤

GAZA STRIP

RED

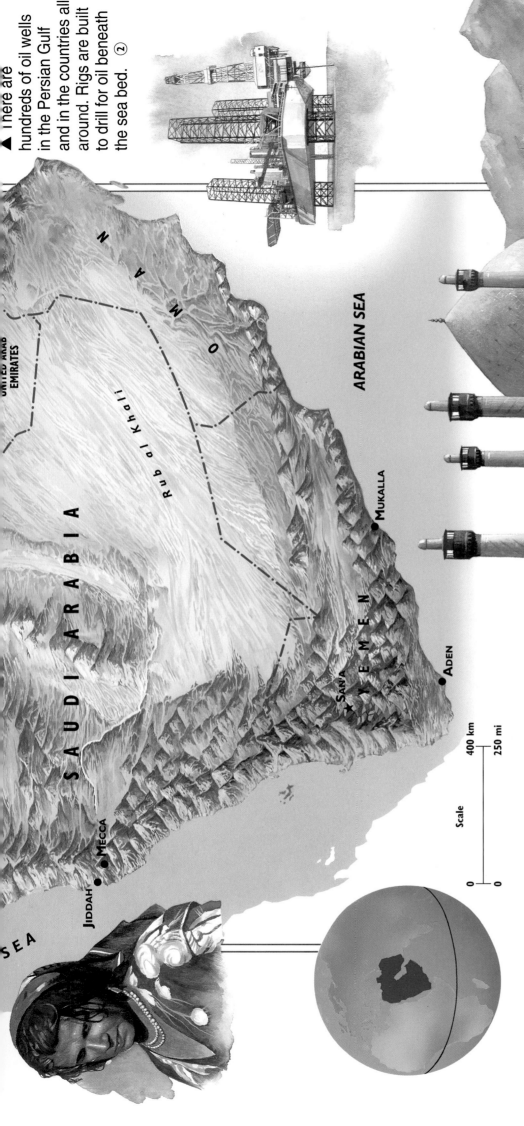

▲ There are hundreds of oil wells in the Persian Gulf and in the countries all around. Rigs are built to drill for oil beneath the sea bed. ②

OMAN

N

SAUDI ARABIA

UNITED ARAB EMIRATES

Rub al Khali

YEMEN

SEA

JIDDAH

MECCA

SAN'A

ADEN

MUKALLA

ARABIAN SEA

Scale

0 — 400 km

0 — 250 mi

▲ This woman is a Kurd. Her people come from the hills of northern Iraq, northwestern Iran, and southeastern Turkey. ④

▲ The royal mosque in Esfahan, Iran, was built 400 years ago by an emperor called Shah Abbas. He ruled over a great empire in the Middle East. He made Esfahan, his capital, one of the largest and most beautiful cities in the world. A mile above sea level on a dry, barren plain, more than one million people lived amongst the tree-lined avenues, parks and bustling bazars. There were 162 mosques (places of Muslim worship) and 273 public baths! ③

SOUTH ASIA

NINETY of the hundred highest peaks in the world are found in the Himalaya and Karakoram mountain ranges. Two great rivers, the Ganges and the Brahmaputra, flow down from the mountains. They meet and form a delta, a great swampy tangle of river mouths, as they enter the sea.

▲ Indian farmworkers take a ride on the roof of a train on its way to Calcutta. The country is crisscrossed by hundreds of railroads. Most were built by the British, who once ruled India. ⑥

▼ If you stand on the roof tops of Kathmandu, capital city of Nepal, this is what you will see. The Himalaya mountains tower all around. ⑤

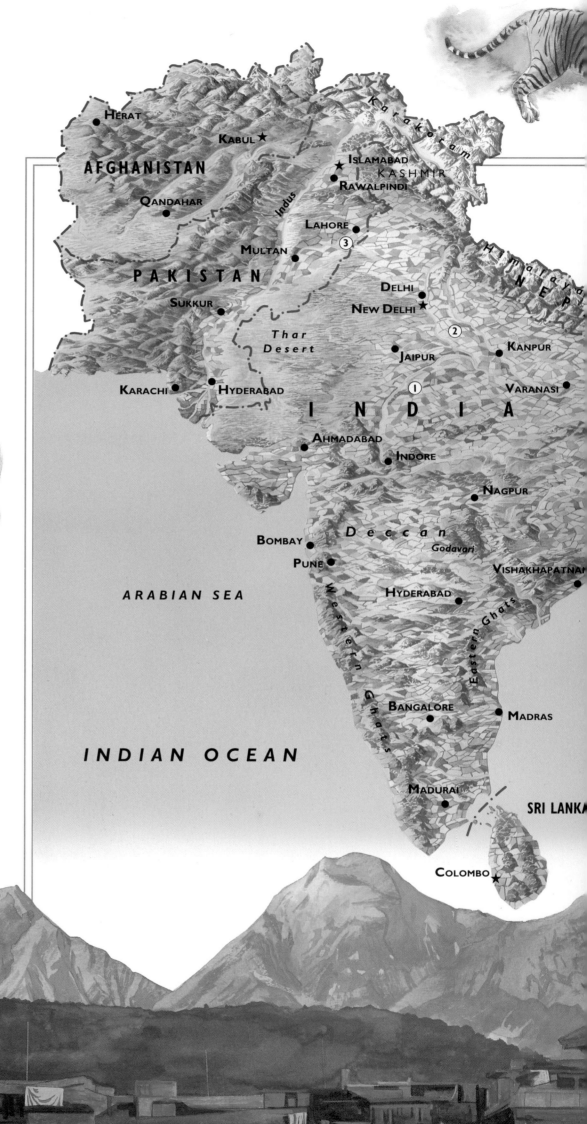

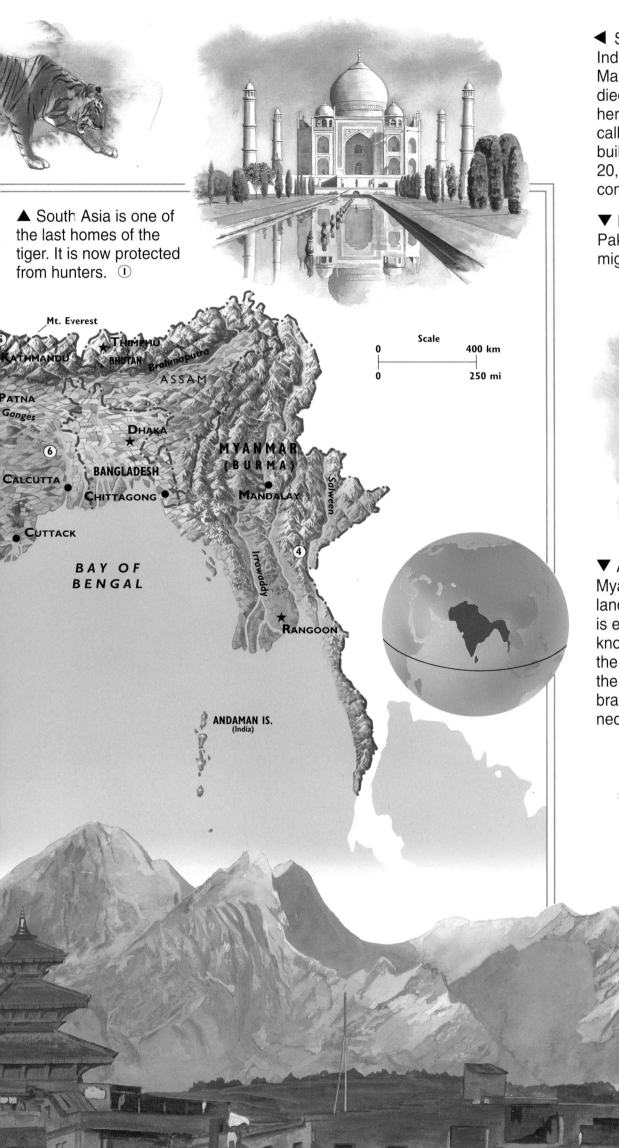

▲ South Asia is one of the last homes of the tiger. It is now protected from hunters. ①

◀ Shah Jahan, emperor of India, loved his wife, Mumtaz Mahal, deeply. When she died, he built the Taj Mahal in her memory. Sometimes called the most beautiful building in the world, it took 20,000 people 20 years to complete. ②

▼ Hail a cab in Lahore, Pakistan, and one of these might stop for you! ③

▼ A corner of southeastern Myanmar is known as the land of the "giraffe women." It is easy to see why they are known by this name! From the age of five years, girls of the Padaung people wear brass rings around their necks, arms, and legs. ④

Mt. Everest

KATHMANDU
THIMPHU
BHUTAN
Brahmaputra
ASSAM

PATNA
Ganges

DHAKA

⑥

BANGLADESH

CALCUTTA
CHITTAGONG

CUTTACK

MYANMAR
(BURMA)

MANDALAY

Salween

Irrawaddy

④

RANGOON

BAY OF BENGAL

ANDAMAN IS.
(India)

Scale

0 ————— 400 km

0 ————— 250 mi

SOUTHEAST ASIA

ALL THE COUNTRIES shown on this map have tropical climates. Most of the year it is very hot and there is a lot of rain. The valleys and plains are packed with rice fields.

Many different peoples live in Southeast Asia. Not so long ago, fierce "headhunter" tribes stalked the rain forests of Borneo and New Guinea.

▲ Children cross over a wooden bridge in southern Vietnam. This part of the country, near the mouth of the Mekong River, is flat and marshy with many rivers. Bridges have to be built on tall stilts to keep clear of floods. ⑦

▶ This is the great temple of Angkor Wat in Cambodia. Eight hundred years ago, a huge city of one million people surrounded this building. It was a very holy place where people came to worship. Now Angkor Wat stands in the middle of a jungle. Parts of it have crumbled away. ⑥

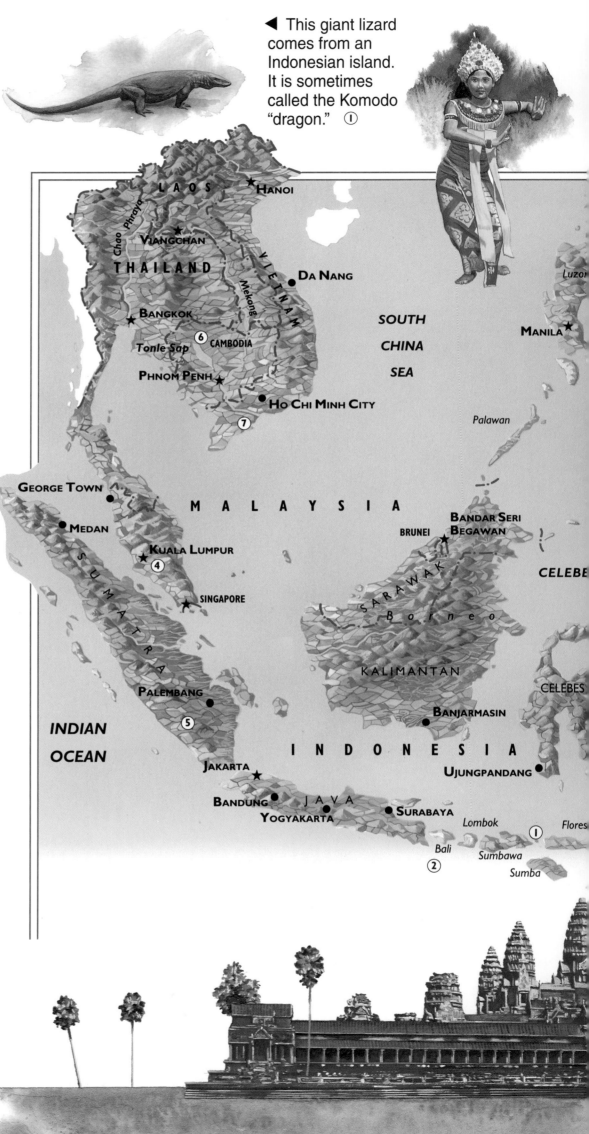

◀ This giant lizard comes from an Indonesian island. It is sometimes called the Komodo "dragon." ①

◄ The island of Bali is famous for its dancers. The girls wear colorful traditional costumes. Their performances delight Bali's many visitors. ②

◄ This village in the Philippines is built in the sea! It is located off the southern tip of the island of Mindanao. The houses stand on stilts in a calm bay called a lagoon. The villagers get most of their food from the sea. Their fishing boats, called *vintas*, have brightly colored sails. ③

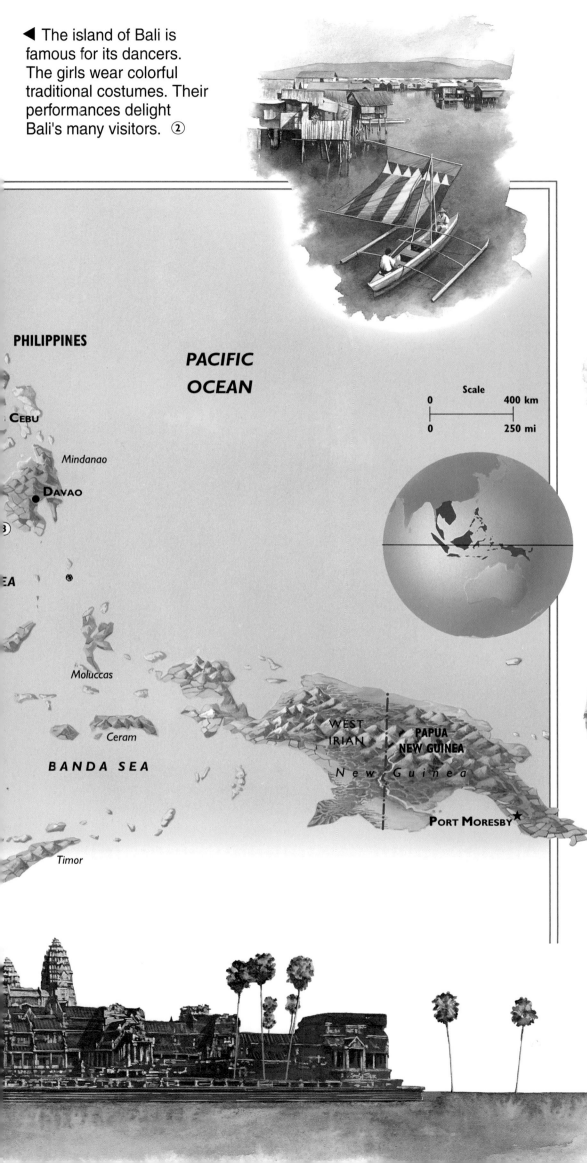

PHILIPPINES

PACIFIC OCEAN

CEBU

Mindanao

● DAVAO

Scale

0   400 km
0   250 mi

Moluccas

Ceram

BANDA SEA

WEST IRIAN

PAPUA NEW GUINEA

New Guinea

PORT MORESBY ★

Timor

▲ A man rides his oxcart through the streets of Kuala Lumpur, capital city of Malaysia. This may soon be a scene of the past. Malaysia is fast becoming a prosperous industrial nation. ④

▲ Many Indonesian islands are still covered with thick tropical rain forest. More different kinds of plants and animals live here than in any other part of the world. This is a picture of *Rafflesia*, the largest flower in the world. Measuring about three feet across, it grows on the island of Sumatra. The petals smell like rotting meat! ⑤

CHINA

VERY FEW people live in western China, a land of high mountains and dry deserts. Eastern China could not be more different. It is home to more than a billion people, one fifth of the world's population. Two great rivers flow across the landscape. They are the Huang He, named the "Yellow River" for the color of the soil in the surrounding countryside, and the Yangtse.

◀ The Great Wall winds more than 2,000 miles across China's hills and valleys. ①

▶ A girl from south China. ②

▲ This bronze statue of a horse is about 12 inches high and 1,800 years old. It was found at a place in central China close to where the Silk Road used to pass. This was an ancient trail that ran from China across Asia to the Middle East. ⑧

Ürümqi

Kashi

Takla Makan

Lop Nor

Yumen

Koko Nor

Himalayas

TIBET

Mt. Everest

Lhasa

Scale
0 — 400 km
0 — 250 mi

▼ The Xi River winds its way past these weirdly shaped hills near Guilin in southern China. ⑦

◀ This farmer goes to market with his load of ducks and chickens for sale. ③

◀ This round building in Beijing, China's capital city, is called the Temple of Heaven. It was built for an emperor nearly 500 years ago. He wished to pray to the gods for a good harvest each year. The temple has four main doors, one for each season. After the Temple was burnt down in a fire 100 years ago, 32 officials were beheaded. ④

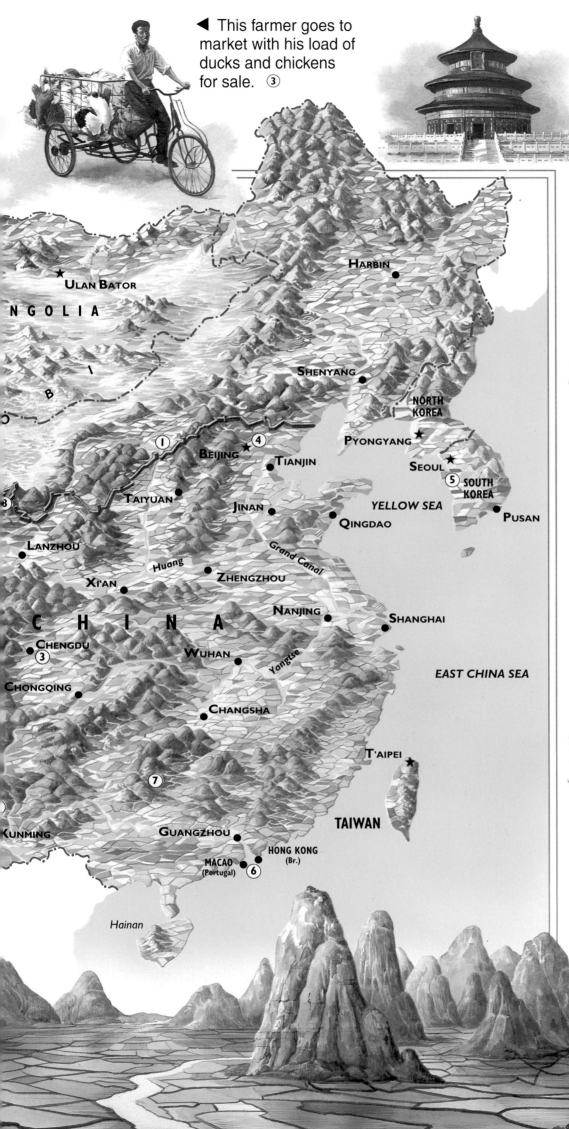

ULAN BATOR

M O N G O L I A

G O B I

HARBIN

SHENYANG

NORTH KOREA

PYONGYANG

① BEIJING ④ TIANJIN

SEOUL ⑤ SOUTH KOREA

PUSAN

TAIYUAN

JINAN

YELLOW SEA

QINGDAO

LANZHOU

Huang

Grand Canal

XI'AN ZHENGZHOU

C H I N A NANJING

SHANGHAI

CHENGDU ③ WUHAN

Yangtse

EAST CHINA SEA

CHONGQING CHANGSHA

T'AIPEI

⑦

TAIWAN

KUNMING GUANGZHOU

MACAO (Portugal) ⑥ HONG KONG (Br.)

Hainan

▲ A funeral procession crosses the fields in South Korea. Although it is now a modern industrial country, many people keep their traditional ways of life. Here, men and women are dressed in white, the Korean color of mourning. The procession is led by people carrying banners. The dead man will be buried in a mound of earth. ⑤

▲ Hong Kong is a large, crowded, modern city. The land close to the harbor bristles with skyscrapers. Hong Kong has for many years been owned by Great Britain. Soon it will once again become part of China. ⑥

JAPAN

FOUR LARGE ISLANDS, and quite a few small ones, make up the country of Japan. The main islands are, in order of size, Honshu, Hokkaido, Kyushu, and Shikoku. Japan is a land of mountain and forest. The few plains and valleys are crammed with rice fields and cities. Japan has very little farmland. The sea is a valuable source of food for

most Japanese. More fish is eaten in Japan than anywhere else in the world. The modern fishing fleet catches more fish than any other country.

Each year, there are about 5,000 earthquakes. Japan would seem to be a dangerous place to live! In fact, most are small ground tremors and go almost unnoticed.

▲ This castle, known as "White Heron," has curved roofs and windows, but no battlements or towers. ①

HOKKAIDO

SAPPORO

HAKODATE

AOMORI

SENDAI

NIIGATA

Scale

0   200 km

0   150 mi

▼ The "Wedded Rocks" stand in the sea off the southern coast of Japan. There is a legend that they are the gods who gave birth to the islands of Japan. ⑥

SEA OF JAPAN

▲ There are many hot springs in Japan. People can bathe in them even on a freezing winter's day! This spring is at Beppu, on the island of Kyushu. ⑦

▶ In Japan, May 5 is called Children's Day. Streamers shaped like fish called carp are flown from the rooftops. ⑤

Once a year, children aged seven, five, or three attend a festival called 7-5-3, or *schichi-go-san*. ②

▲ The Japanese write using simple pictures, called characters, instead of our alphabet. This boy is learning to write well. ③

平和日本

TOKYO ★

YOKOHAMA

Mt. Fuji

NAGOYA

KYOTO

OSAKA

KOBE

WAKAYAMA

OKAYAMA

HIROSHIMA

TAKAMATSU

MATSUYAMA

SHIKOKU

KITAKYUSHU

FUKUOKA

NAGASAKI

MIYAZAKI

KYUSHU

PACIFIC OCEAN

▼ A high-speed train, named the "bullet train" for the shape of its nose, whistles past Mount Fuji. ④

Ryukyu Islands

Okinawa

NATIONS OF OCEANIA

AUSTRALIA
Area 2,966,155 sq mi **Population** 17,292,000
Capital Canberra **Language** English

FIJI
Area 7,056 sq mi **Population** 746,000
Capital Suva **Languages** Fijian, Hindi, English

KIRIBATI
Area 313 sq mi **Population** 72,000
Capital Bairiki **Languages** I-Kiribati, English

MARSHALL ISLANDS
Area 70 sq mi **Population** 43,000
Capital Majuro **Language** English

◄ Boy from Solomon Islands ①

▲ Australian boy ③

NAURU
Area 8 sq mi **Population** 9,000 **Capital** Yaren
District **Languages** Nauruan, English

NEW ZEALAND
Area 104,454 sq mi **Population** 3,455,000
Capital Wellington **Languages** English, Maori

▲ Maori girl, from New Zealand ②

PAPUA NEW GUINEA
Area 178,704 sq mi **Pop.** 3,772,000 **Capital** Port
Moresby **Languages** Pidgin, English, Motu

SOLOMON ISLANDS
Area 10,954 sq mi **Population** 319,000 **Capital**
Honiara **Languages** English, Pidgin

TONGA
Area 288 sq mi **Population** 103,000 **Capital**
Nuku'alofa **Languages** Tongan, English

AUSTRALIA

PAPUA NEW GUINEA

NAURU

KIRIBATI

SOLOMON ISLANDS

VANUATU

TUVALU

FIJI

WESTERN SAMOA

TONGA

NEW ZEALAND

OCEANIA

OCEANIA is the name given to the group of countries located in the South Pacific. It is made up of Australia (itself an island continent), New Zealand, Papua New Guinea, and the islands of the Pacific Ocean. (For a complete map of the Pacific islands see pages 6-7).

Human beings probably first arrived in Australia more than 50,000 years ago. Perhaps the first peoples to travel by sea, they came from Southeast Asia. Thousands of years later, people reached the Pacific Islands and New Zealand in their sturdy oceangoing canoes.

Ore train

ng Doctor

Saltwater crocodile

Great Barrier Reef

Snorkeling

Spiny anteater

Mining

QUEENSLAND

Sugar cane

Kangaroo

Cattle

Koala

Spinifex grass

A L I A

L. Eyre

Darling

SOUTH

STRALIA

Shepherd

Wheat

Mining

NEW SOUTH WALES

Coal

Grapes

Sheep

Grapes

Murray

VICTORIA

Sheep

Gas tanker

Duckbilled platypus

TASMANIA

Sperm whale

TASMAN SEA

Cattle

Kiwi

NEW ZEALAND

Mt. Cook

Kakapo

Sheep

Sheep

FACTS ABOUT OCEANIA

Area 3,444,278 sq mi
Population 26,700,000
Highest point Mt. Cook (New Zealand) 12,349 ft
Lowest point Lake Eyre (Australia) 52 ft below sea level
Longest river Murray-Darling (Australia) 2,330 mi
Largest lake Lake Eyre (Australia) 3,700 sq mi
Largest country Australia 2,966,155 sq mi
Largest population Australia 17,292,000
Largest city Sydney (Australia) 3,623,500

TUVALU
Area 10 sq mi **Population** 10,000 **Capital** Funafuti **Languages** Tuvaluan, English

VANUATU
Area 4,707 sq mi **Population** 157,000 **Capital** Port Vila **Languages** Bislama, English, French

WESTERN SAMOA
Area 1,093 sq mi **Population** 197,000 **Capital** Apia **Languages** Samoan, English

AUSTRALIA

AUSTRALIA is about the same area as the United States (excluding Alaska). Its population is only a tiny fraction of that country's. Much of the land in the west, covered by grass and low bushes, is dry scrub, known as the "bush." Most people live in the southeast.

▲ Sydney is Australia's largest city. It is located in the southeast of the country, where most Australians live. Sydney is famous for two magnificent landmarks: the Opera House and Harbor Bridge. The roof of the Opera House was built to look like the sails of yachts on the harbor waters. The bridge, which carries both trains and cars, is known to local people as the "Coathanger!" ⑦

◄ Daubed in white body paint, this Aborigine performs a traditional dance. Aborigines have lived in Australia for thousands of years. ①

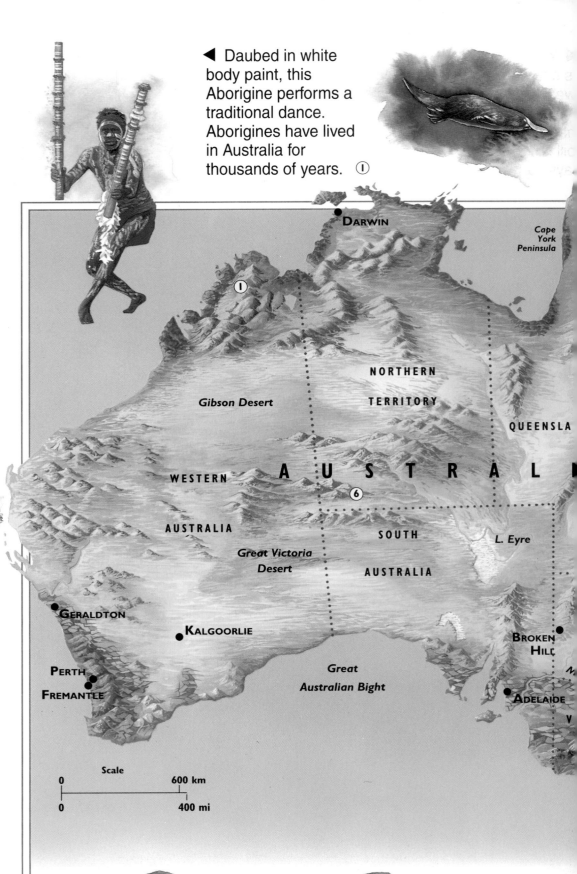

DARWIN

Cape York Peninsula

①

NORTHERN

TERRITORY

Gibson Desert

QUEENSLA

WESTERN

A U S T R A L I

⑥

AUSTRALIA

SOUTH

L. Eyre

Great Victoria Desert

AUSTRALIA

GERALDTON

KALGOORLIE

BROKEN HILL

PERTH

Great Australian Bight

FREMANTLE

ADELAIDE

Scale

0   600 km

0   400 mi

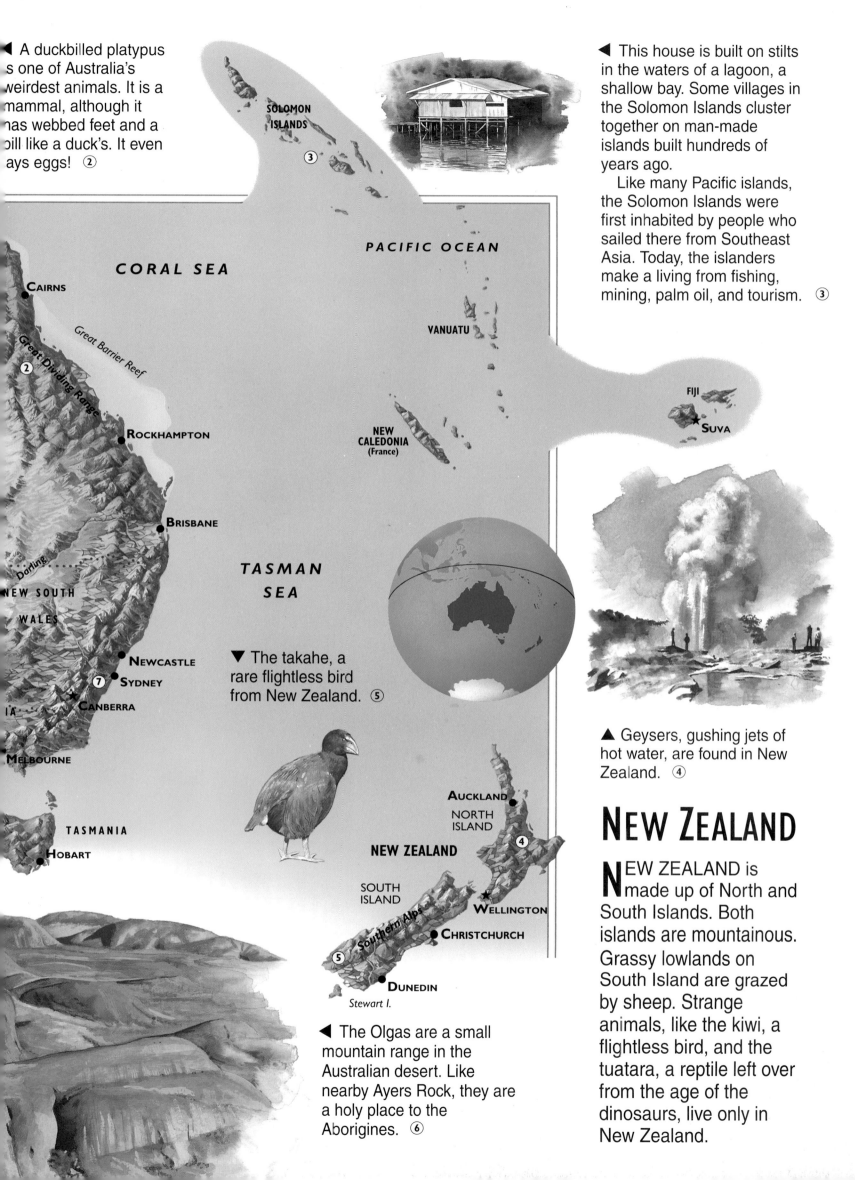

◀ A duckbilled platypus is one of Australia's weirdest animals. It is a mammal, although it has webbed feet and a bill like a duck's. It even lays eggs! ②

◀ This house is built on stilts in the waters of a lagoon, a shallow bay. Some villages in the Solomon Islands cluster together on man-made islands built hundreds of years ago.

Like many Pacific islands, the Solomon Islands were first inhabited by people who sailed there from Southeast Asia. Today, the islanders make a living from fishing, mining, palm oil, and tourism. ③

SOLOMON ISLANDS

PACIFIC OCEAN

CORAL SEA

CAIRNS

Great Barrier Reef

Great Dividing Range

②

ROCKHAMPTON

BRISBANE

Darling

NEW SOUTH WALES

TASMAN SEA

VANUATU

NEW CALEDONIA (France)

FIJI

SUVA

▼ The takahe, a rare flightless bird from New Zealand. ⑤

NEWCASTLE

⑦ SYDNEY

CANBERRA

IA

MELBOURNE

TASMANIA

HOBART

AUCKLAND

NORTH ISLAND

NEW ZEALAND

SOUTH ISLAND

Southern Alps

WELLINGTON

CHRISTCHURCH

⑤

DUNEDIN

Stewart I.

④

▲ Geysers, gushing jets of hot water, are found in New Zealand. ④

NEW ZEALAND

NEW ZEALAND is made up of North and South Islands. Both islands are mountainous. Grassy lowlands on South Island are grazed by sheep. Strange animals, like the kiwi, a flightless bird, and the tuatara, a reptile left over from the age of the dinosaurs, live only in New Zealand.

◀ The Olgas are a small mountain range in the Australian desert. Like nearby Ayers Rock, they are a holy place to the Aborigines. ⑥

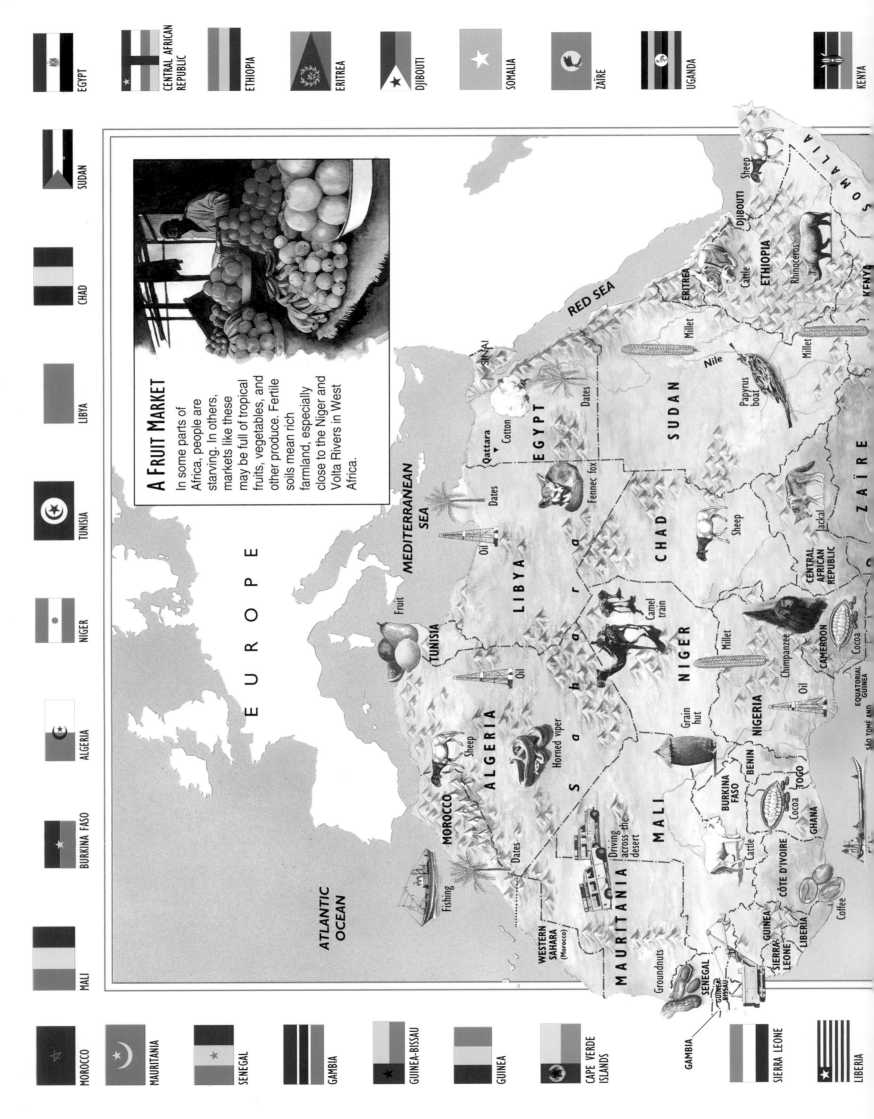

68

EGYPT

CENTRAL AFRICAN REPUBLIC

ETHIOPIA

ERITREA

DJIBOUTI

SOMALIA

ZAÏRE

UGANDA

KENYA

SUDAN

CHAD

LIBYA

TUNISIA

NIGER

ALGERIA

BURKINA FASO

MALI

MOROCCO

MAURITANIA

SENEGAL

GAMBIA

GUINEA-BISSAU

GUINEA

CAPE VERDE ISLANDS

SIERRA LEONE

LIBERIA

A Fruit Market

In some parts of Africa, people are starving. In others, markets like these may be full of tropical fruits, vegetables, and other produce. Fertile soils mean rich farmland, especially close to the Niger and Volta Rivers in West Africa.

MEDITERRANEAN SEA

RED SEA

EUROPE

ATLANTIC OCEAN

SINAI

Qattara

Cotton

EGYPT

Dates

Oil

LIBYA

Fruit

TUNISIA

Oil

Fennec fox

Sheep

S a h a r a

Horned viper

ALGERIA

MOROCCO

Dates

Fishing

WESTERN SAHARA (Morocco)

Driving across the desert

MAURITANIA

MALI

Groundnuts

SENEGAL

GAMBIA

GUINEA-BISSAU

Nile

Papyrus boat

SUDAN

Millet

Camel train

Jackal

CHAD

NIGER

Millet

Grain hut

Cattle

BURKINA FASO

BENIN

NIGERIA

Oil

CENTRAL AFRICAN REPUBLIC

Chimpanzee

CAMEROON

Cocoa

EQUATORIAL GUINEA

SÃO TOMÉ AND

TOGO

Cocoa

GHANA

CÔTE D'IVOIRE

Coffee

GUINEA

SIERRA LEONE

LIBERIA

ZAÏRE

Millet

Sheep

Cattle

Rhinoceros

ETHIOPIA

ERITREA

DJIBOUTI

SOMALIA

KENYA

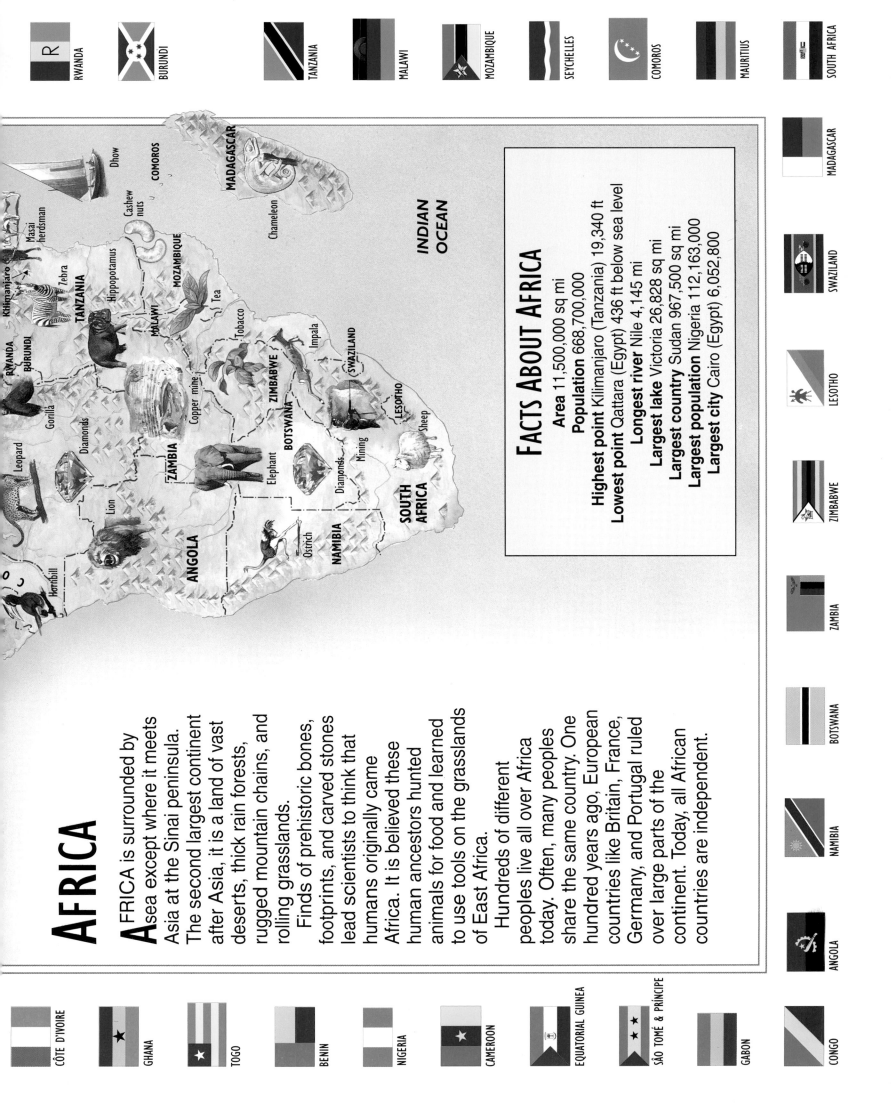

AFRICA

AFRICA is surrounded by a sea except where it meets Asia at the Sinai peninsula. The second largest continent after Asia, it is a land of vast deserts, thick rain forests, rugged mountain chains, and rolling grasslands.

Finds of prehistoric bones, footprints, and carved stones lead scientists to think that humans originally came from Africa. It is believed these human ancestors hunted animals for food and learned to use tools on the grasslands of East Africa.

Hundreds of different peoples live all over Africa today. Often, many peoples share the same country. One hundred years ago, European countries like Britain, France, Germany, and Portugal ruled over large parts of the continent. Today, all African countries are independent.

FACTS ABOUT AFRICA

Area 11,500,000 sq mi
Population 668,700,000
Highest point Kilimanjaro (Tanzania) 19,340 ft
Lowest point Qattara (Egypt) 436 ft below sea level
Longest river Nile 4,145 mi
Largest lake Victoria 26,828 sq mi
Largest country Sudan 967,500 sq mi
Largest population Nigeria 112,163,000
Largest city Cairo (Egypt) 6,052,800

Flags: RWANDA, BURUNDI, TANZANIA, MALAWI, MOZAMBIQUE, SEYCHELLES, COMOROS, MAURITIUS, SOUTH AFRICA, MADAGASCAR, SWAZILAND, LESOTHO, ZIMBABWE, ZAMBIA, BOTSWANA, NAMIBIA, ANGOLA, CONGO, GABON, SÃO TOMÉ & PRÍNCIPE, EQUATORIAL GUINEA, CAMEROON, NIGERIA, BENIN, TOGO, GHANA, CÔTE D'IVOIRE

Map labels: Dhow, COMOROS, MADAGASCAR, Cashew nuts, Chameleon, Masai herdsman, Kilimanjaro, Zebra, Hippopotamus, TANZANIA, MOZAMBIQUE, Tea, Tobacco, MALAWI, Impala, Copper mine, ZIMBABWE, SWAZILAND, LESOTHO, Sheep, BOTSWANA, Mining, Diamonds, SOUTH AFRICA, Elephant, Ostrich, NAMIBIA, ANGOLA, Lion, Diamonds, Leopard, Gorilla, RWANDA, BURUNDI, ZAMBIA, Hornbill, INDIAN OCEAN

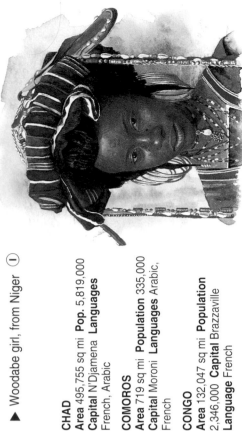

NATIONS OF AFRICA

ALGERIA
Area 919,515 sq mi **Pop.** 25,660,000 **Capital** Algiers **Languages** Arabic, French

ANGOLA
Area 481,354 sq mi **Pop.** 10,303,000 **Capital** Luanda **Languages** Portuguese, Bantu languages

BENIN
Area 43,475 sq mi **Population** 4,889,000 **Capital** Porto-Novo **Language** French

BOTSWANA
Area 224,711 sq mi **Pop.** 1,348,000 **Capital** Gaborone **Languages** English, Tswana

BURKINA FASO
Area 105,869 sq mi **Pop.** 9,242,000 **Capital** Ouagadougou **Languages** French, Mossi

BURUNDI
Area 10,747 sq mi **Pop.** 5,620,000 **Capital** Bujumbura **Languages** French, Kirundi, Swahili

CAMEROON
Area 183,569 sq mi **Pop.** 12,239,000 **Capital** Yaoundé **Languages** French, English

CAPE VERDE ISLANDS
Area 1,557 sq mi **Pop.** 370,000 **Capital** Praia **Languages** Portuguese, Crioulo

CENTRAL AFRICAN REPUBLIC
Area 240,535 sq mi **Pop.** 3,127,000 **Capital** Bangui **Languages** French, Sango

CÔTE D'IVOIRE
Area 124,518 sq mi **Pop.** 13,765,000 **Capitals** Yamoussoukro, Abidjan **Languages** French, Malinke

DJIBOUTI
Area 8,958 sq mi **Pop.** 520,000 **Capital** Djibouti **Languages** Arabic, French

EGYPT
Area 386,662 sq mi **Pop.** 54,688,000 **Capital** Cairo **Language** Arabic

EQUATORIAL GUINEA
Area 10,831 sq mi **Pop.** 356,000 **Capital** Malabo **Language** Spanish

ERITREA
Area 93,679 sq mi **Pop.** 2,000,000 **Capital** Asmera **Language** Tigrinya

ETHIOPIA
Area 435,609 sq mi **Pop.** 49,883,000 **Capital** Addis Ababa **Language** Amharic

CHAD
Area 495,755 sq mi **Pop.** 5,819,000 **Capital** N'Djamena **Languages** French, Arabic

COMOROS
Area 719 sq mi **Population** 335,000 **Capital** Moroni **Languages** Arabic, French

CONGO
Area 132,047 sq mi **Population** 2,346,000 **Capital** Brazzaville **Language** French

▲ Woodabe girl, from Niger ①

GABON
Area 103,347 sq mi **Pop.** 1,212,000 **Capital** Libreville **Languages** French, Fang, Bantu languages

GAMBIA
Area 4,127 sq mi **Pop.** 884,000 **Capital** Banjul **Language** English

GHANA
Area 92,098 sq mi **Pop.** 16,445,000 **Capital** Accra **Languages** English, Kwa languages

GUINEA
Area 94,926 sq mi **Pop.** 5,931,000 **Capital** Conakry **Languages** French, Soussou, Manika

GUINEA-BISSAU
Area 13,948 sq mi **Pop.** 984,000 **Capital** Bissau **Language** Portuguese

▲ Berber girl from Morocco ⑥

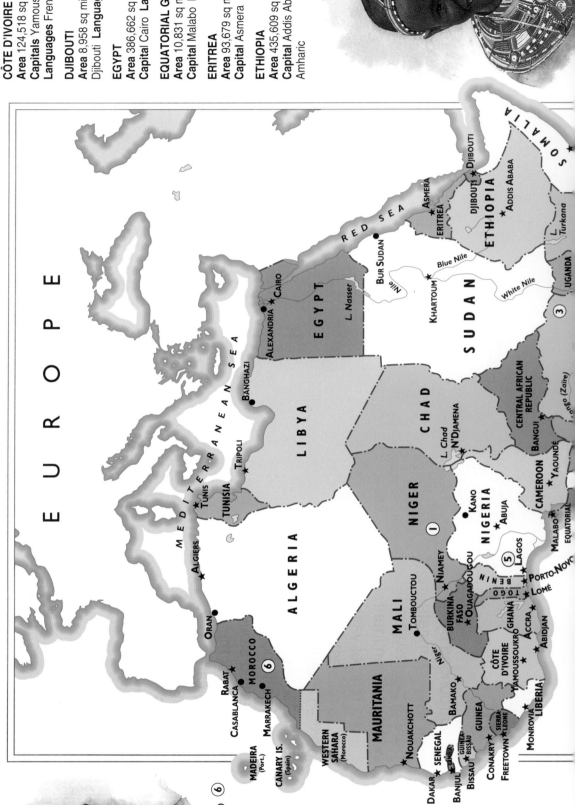

EUROPE

MEDITERRANEAN SEA

RED SEA

SOMALIA

ALEXANDRIA
CAIRO
L. Nasser
EGYPT

SUDAN
KHARTOUM
Blue Nile
White Nile
Nile
BUR SUDAN

ETHIOPIA
ADDIS ABABA
DJIBOUTI
DJIBOUTI
ERITREA
ASMERA
Turkana
UGANDA
③

BANGHAZI
TRIPOLI
TUNIS
TUNISIA
LIBYA
CHAD
L. Chad
N'DJAMENA

ALGIERS
ALGERIA
NIGER
NIAMEY
①
NIGERIA
KANO
ABUJA
LAGOS ⑤
CENTRAL AFRICAN REPUBLIC
BANGUI
CAMEROON
YAOUNDÉ
EQUATORIAL
MALABO
Congo (Zaire)

ORAN
MOROCCO ⑥
RABAT
CASABLANCA
MARRAKECH
WESTERN SAHARA (Morocco)
MAURITANIA
NOUAKCHOTT
MALI
TOMBOUCTOU
BAMAKO
Niger
BURKINA FASO
OUAGADOUGOU
BENIN
TOGO
GHANA
ACCRA
LOMÉ
PORTO-NOVO
CÔTE D'IVOIRE
YAMOUSSOUKRO
ABIDJAN
LIBERIA
MONROVIA

MADEIRA (Port.)
CANARY IS. (Spain)

DAKAR
SENEGAL
GUINEA-BISSAU
BANJUL
BISSAU
CONAKRY
GUINEA
SIERRA LEONE
FREETOWN

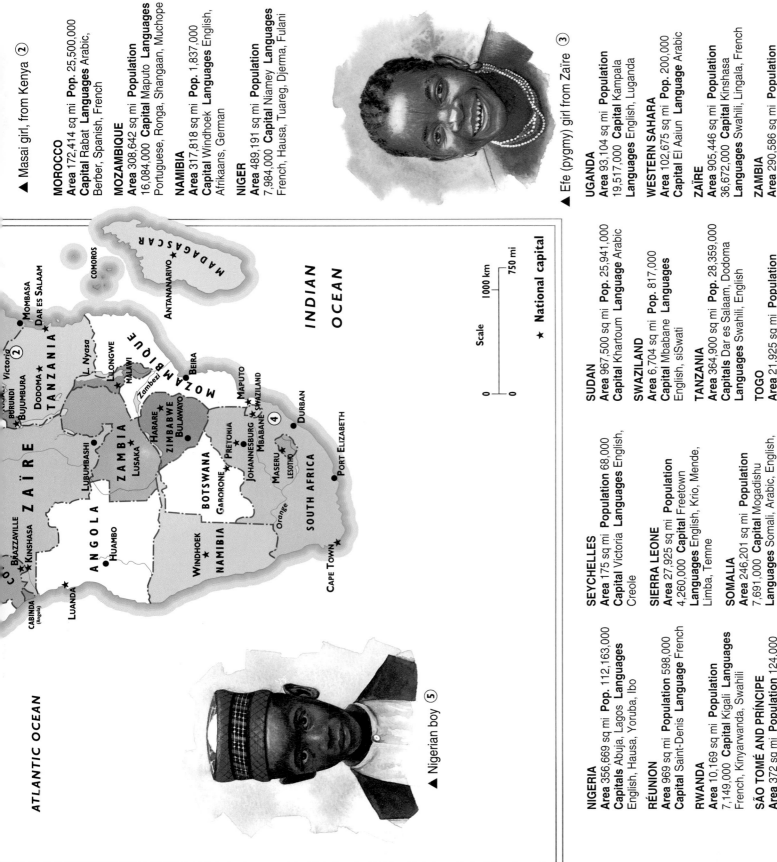

▲ Masai girl, from Kenya ②

MOROCCO
Area 172,414 sq mi **Pop.** 25,500,000
Capital Rabat **Languages** Arabic,
Berber, Spanish, French

MOZAMBIQUE
Area 308,642 sq mi **Capital** Maputo **Languages**
16,084,000 Portuguese, Ronga, Shangaan, Muchope

NAMIBIA
Area 317,818 sq mi **Pop.** 1,837,000
Capital Windhoek **Languages** English,
Afrikaans, German

NIGER
Area 489,191 sq mi **Population**
7,984,000 **Capital** Niamey **Languages**
French, Hausa, Tuareg, Djerma, Fulani

▲ Efe (pygmy) girl from Zaïre ③

UGANDA
Area 93,104 sq mi **Population**
19,517,000 **Capital** Kampala
Languages English, Luganda

WESTERN SAHARA
Area 102,675 sq mi **Pop.** 200,000
Capital El Aaiun **Language** Arabic

ZAÏRE
Area 905,446 sq mi **Population**
36,672,000 **Capital** Kinshasa
Languages Swahili, Lingala, French

ZAMBIA
Area 290,586 sq mi **Population**
8,780,000 **Capital** Lusaka
Languages English, Lozi

ZIMBABWE
Area 150,873,000 sq mi **Population**
10,412,000 **Capital** Harare
Languages English, Shona, Ndebele

ATLANTIC OCEAN

MADAGASCAR

COMOROS

MOMBASA
DAR ES SALAAM

Victoria ②
L. Nyasa
DODOMA ★
TANZANIA
LILONGWE
MALAWI ★
Zambezi
MOZAMBIQUE
BEIRA
MAPUTO

BUJUMBURA
BURUNDI ★

ZAÏRE

HARARE ★
BULAWAYO
ZIMBABWE
LUSAKA ★
ZAMBIA
LUBUMBASHI

ANTANANARIVO ★

MADAGASCAR

INDIAN
OCEAN

PRETORIA ★
JOHANNESBURG ●
MASERU
MBABANE ★ SWAZILAND
LESOTHO ★
SOUTH AFRICA
DURBAN
PORT ELIZABETH

GABORONE ★
BOTSWANA

Orange

WINDHOEK ★
NAMIBIA
ANGOLA

HUAMBO ●

CABINDA
(Angola)
LUANDA ★

BRAZZAVILLE
KINSHASA ★

Scale

0   1000 km
0   750 mi

★ National capital

SEYCHELLES
Area 175 sq mi **Population** 68,000
Capital Victoria **Languages** English,
Creole

SIERRA LEONE
Area 27,925 sq mi **Population**
4,260,000 **Capital** Freetown
Languages English, Krio, Mende,
Limba, Temne

SOMALIA
Area 246,201 sq mi **Population**
7,691,000 **Capital** Mogadishu
Languages Somali, Arabic, English,
Italian

SOUTH AFRICA
Area 433,680 sq mi **Pop.** 36,070,000
Capitals Pretoria, Cape Town
Languages Afrikaans, English, Xhosa,
Zulu, Sesotho

SUDAN
Area 967,500 sq mi **Pop.** 25,941,000
Capital Khartoum **Language** Arabic

SWAZILAND
Area 6,704 sq mi **Pop.** 817,000
Capital Mbabane **Languages**
English, siSwati

TANZANIA
Area 364,900 sq mi **Pop.** 28,359,000
Capitals Dar es Salaam, Dodoma
Languages Swahili, English

TOGO
Area 21,925 sq mi **Population**
3,643,000 **Capital** Lome **Languages**
French, Kabiye, Ewe

TUNISIA
Area 63,170 sq mi **Population**
8,362,000 **Capital** Tunis **Languages**
Arabic, Berber, French

▲ Nigerian boy ⑤

NIGERIA
Area 356,669 sq mi **Pop.** 112,163,000
Capitals Abuja, Lagos **Languages**
English, Hausa, Yoruba, Ibo

RÉUNION
Area 969 sq mi **Population** 598,000
Capital Saint-Denis **Language** French

RWANDA
Area 10,169 sq mi **Population**
7,149,000 **Capital** Kigali **Languages**
French, Kinyarwanda, Swahili

SÃO TOMÉ AND PRÍNCIPE
Area 372 sq mi **Population** 124,000
Capital São Tomé **Language**
Portuguese

SENEGAL
Area 75,951 sq mi **Population**
7,533,000 **Capital** Dakar **Language**
French

KENYA
Area 224,961 sq mi **Pop.** 25,905,000
Capital Nairobi **Languages** Swahili,
English, Kikuyu, Luo

LESOTHO
Area 11,720 sq mi **Pop.** 1,826,000
Capital Maseru **Languages** English,
Sesotho

LIBERIA
Area 38,250 sq mi **Population** 2,705,000
Capital Monrovia **Language** English

LIBYA
Area 679,362 sq mi **Pop.** 4,712,000
Capital Tripoli **Language** Arabic

MADAGASCAR
Area 226,658 sq mi **Pop.** 11,493,000
Capital Antananarivo **Languages**
Malagasy, French

MALAWI
Area 45,747 sq mi **Pop.** 8,556,000
Capital Lilongwe **Languages** English,
Chichewa

MALI
Area 482,077 sq mi **Population**
9,507,000 **Capital** Bamako **Language**
French

MAURITANIA
Area 395,956 sq mi **Pop.** 2,036,000
Capital Nouakchott **Languages** Arabic,
Poular, Wolof, Solinke

MAURITIUS
Area 788 sq mi **Population** 1,059,000
Capital Port Louis **Languages** English,
Creole

▲ Zulu boy, from South Africa ④

NORTHERN AFRICA

A LARGE PART of this map shows an area where hardly anybody lives. All the year round the Sahara Desert is hot and dry. Nothing grows in the bare, stony ground. You may think of a desert as rolling sand dunes, but only parts of the Sahara are sandy. Some areas are quite mountainous.

Farmland and pastures lie to the south. But this area, called the Sahel, is sometimes almost as dry as a desert. Crops cannot grow and grazing animals die.

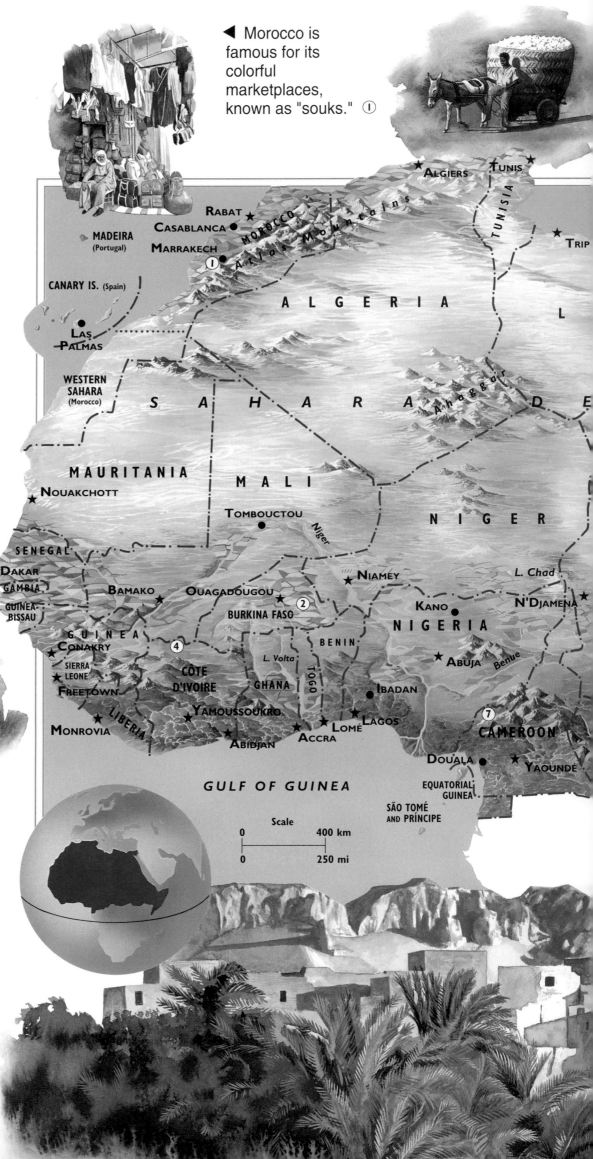

◄ Morocco is famous for its colorful marketplaces, known as "souks." ①

ALGIERS TUNIS
TUNISIA
RABAT
Morocco
CASABLANCA
MADEIRA (Portugal)
MARRAKECH ① Atlas Mountains TRIP
ALGERIA L
CANARY IS. (Spain)
LAS PALMAS
S A H A R A Ahaggar DE
WESTERN SAHARA (Morocco)
MAURITANIA MALI
NOUAKCHOTT
TOMBOUCTOU NIGER
Niger
NIAMEY L. Chad
SENEGAL
DAKAR BAMAKO OUAGADOUGOU KANO N'DJAMENA
GAMBIA ② BURKINA FASO NIGERIA
GUINEA-BISSAU
GUINEA ④ BENIN ABUJA Benue
CONAKRY L. Volta
SIERRA LEONE CÔTE D'IVOIRE GHANA IBADAN ⑦
FREETOWN TOGO LOMÉ LAGOS CAMEROON
YAMOUSSOUKRO ACCRA DOUALA
MONROVIA LIBERIA ABIDJAN YAOUNDÉ
EQUATORIAL GUINEA
GULF OF GUINEA
SÃO TOMÉ AND PRÍNCIPE

Scale
0 400 km
0 250 mi

▲ The people of West Africa dress up in style for special occasions! This man is wearing a hat made of parrot feathers and an elephant mask (note the large ears and long trunk). He wears this costume to show how wealthy and powerful he is. ⑦

◀ This boy from Burkina Faso, in West Africa, drives his donkey cart with a fresh crop of cotton on the back. ②

◀ These are statues of King Ramses II, who ruled in Egypt 3,000 years ago. They are cut out of a rock face at Abu Simbel. A land of great pyramids and temples, ancient Egypt grew up on the rich farmlands close to the banks of the Nile River. ③

▲ This is part of a village in Côte d'Ivoire, West Africa. The round houses are made from baked mud and dried reeds. ④

▼ The Dinka people from Sudan are among the tallest peoples in the world. They spend nearly all their lives tending their herds of cattle. ⑤

◀ Dotted about the Sahara Desert are places where water gushes and palm trees grow. These are called oases. Very often towns are built at these oases, like this one in Egypt. The tall tower is a minaret. From here, a man calls people to come to the mosque for prayer. ⑥

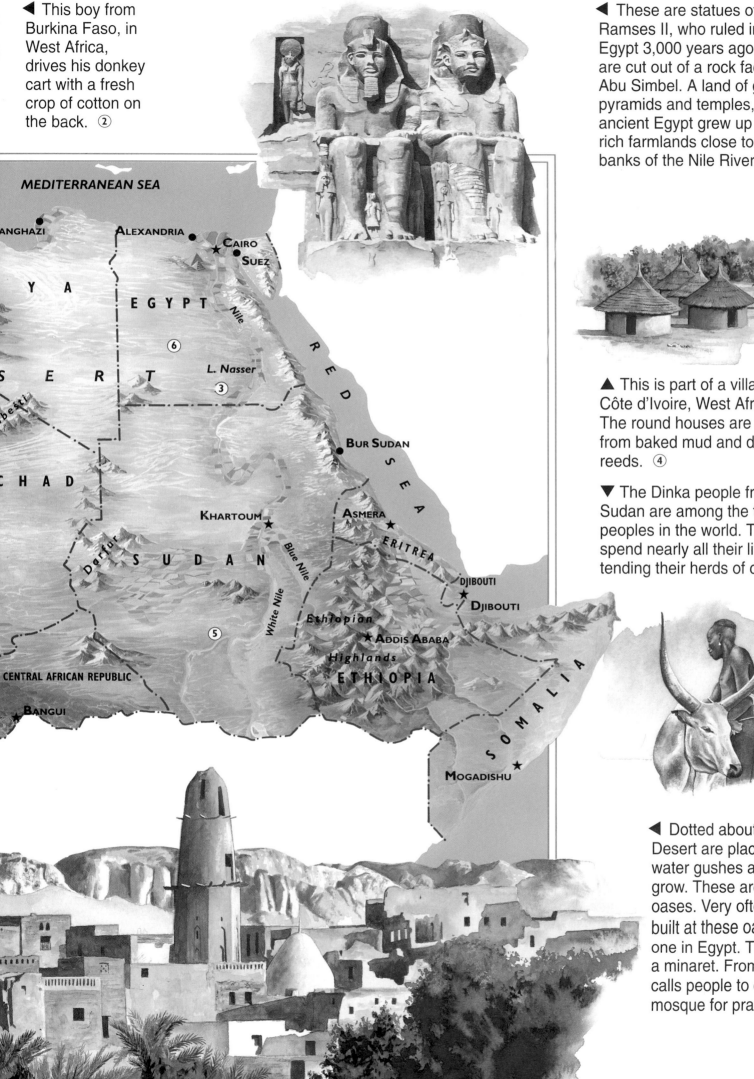

MEDITERRANEAN SEA

ANGHAZI

ALEXANDRIA

CAIRO
SUEZ

EGYPT

Nile

⑥

L. Nasser

③

RED SEA

BUR SUDAN

Tibesti

CHAD

KHARTOUM

ASMERA

ERITREA

Darfur

SUDAN

Blue Nile

White Nile

DJIBOUTI
DJIBOUTI

CENTRAL AFRICAN REPUBLIC

⑤

Ethiopian

ADDIS ABABA

Highlands

ETHIOPIA

SOMALIA

BANGUI

MOGADISHU

SOUTHERN AFRICA

THE SOUTHERN HALF of the African continent is very different from the northern half. There are rain forests, grasslands, known as the savanna, and high mountain ranges.

The savanna is one of the few places in the world where enormous herds of animals still wander freely. Giraffes, wildebeest, zebras, elephants, and others move about the plains feeding on grass and leaves. Lions, cheetahs, and hyenas live on the savanna, too, preying on these grazing animals.

The Bantu people, herdsmen and farmers, traveled from western to southern Africa hundreds of years ago and made it their home. Europeans and Asians have also settled here.

▲ The giraffe is the tallest animal in the world. It feeds on the leaves in the trees of the savanna. ①

▲ This woman is from Mozambique. She rubs a cream made from crushed bark into her skin to keep it moist in the hot sun. ②

▼ The Victoria Falls were named by David Livingstone, the Scottish explorer. ⑦

▲ Elephants and rhinos are killed by poachers, who then cut off and sell their tusks and horns. ⑥

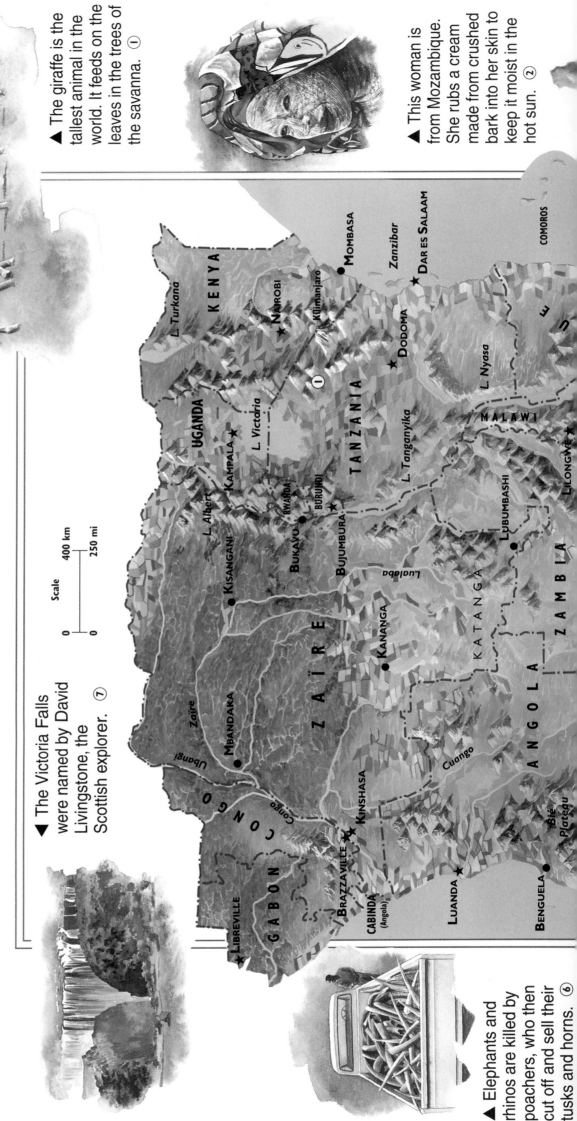

Scale
0   400 km
0   250 mi

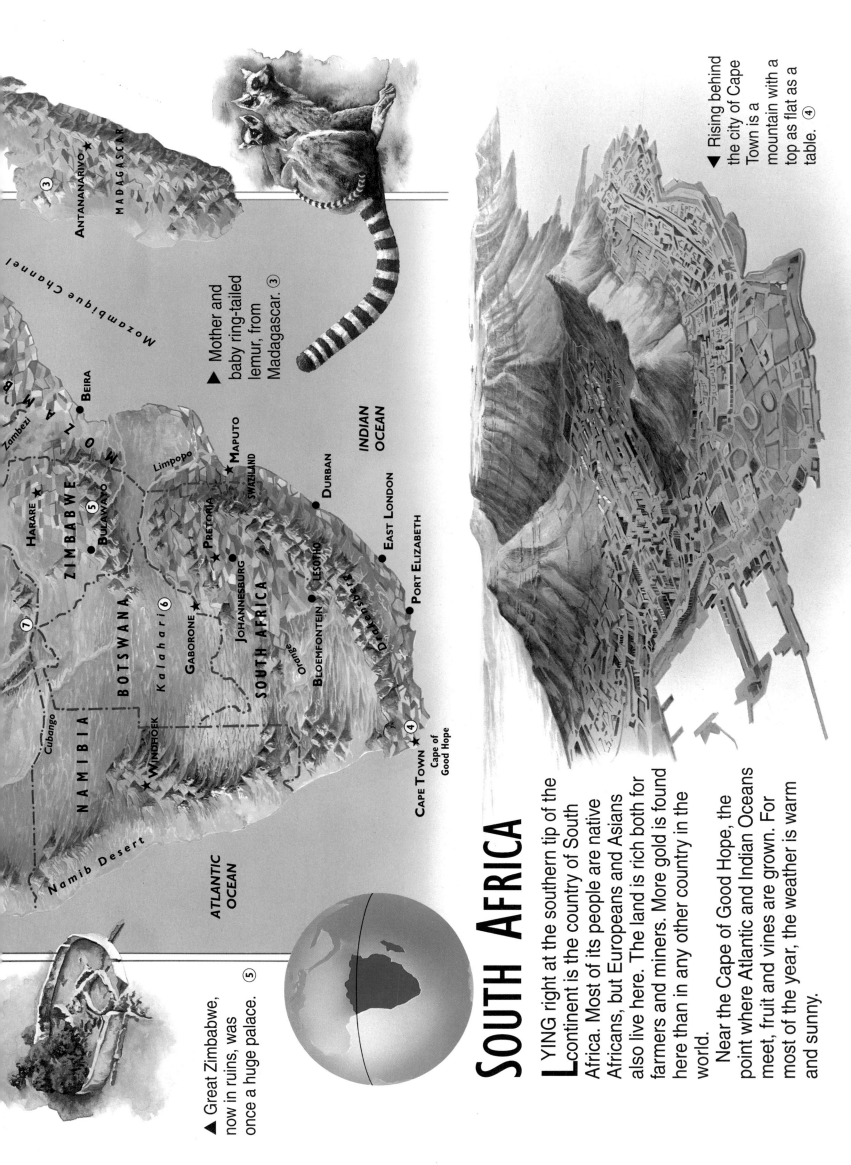

▲ Great Zimbabwe, now in ruins, was once a huge palace. ⑤

▲ Mother and baby ring-tailed lemur, from Madagascar. ③

Mozambique Channel

MADAGASCAR

③ ANTANANARIVO

BEIRA

Zambezi

HARARE

ZIMBABWE

BULAWAYO ⑤

Limpopo

MAPUTO

SWAZILAND

PRETORIA

JOHANNESBURG

BOTSWANA

Kalahari

GABORONE ⑥

SOUTH AFRICA

Orange

BLOEMFONTEIN

LESOTHO

DURBAN

INDIAN OCEAN

EAST LONDON

PORT ELIZABETH

Drakensberg

NAMIBIA

WINDHOEK

Cubango

⑦

Namib Desert

ATLANTIC OCEAN

CAPE TOWN ④
Cape of Good Hope

▼ Rising behind the city of Cape Town is a mountain with a top as flat as a table. ④

SOUTH AFRICA

LYING right at the southern tip of the continent is the country of South Africa. Most of its people are native Africans, but Europeans and Asians also live here. The land is rich both for farmers and miners. More gold is found here than in any other country in the world.

Near the Cape of Good Hope, the point where Atlantic and Indian Oceans meet, fruit and vines are grown. For most of the year, the weather is warm and sunny.

THE POLES

BOTH the North Pole in the Arctic and the South Pole in the Antarctic are bitterly cold places, always covered with ice and snow. The Arctic is quite different from the Antarctic in one important way. It is not land at all, but an ocean covered by a vast frozen cap of thick ice. Antarctica is a continent, like Asia or Africa. Beneath the ice, more than two miles deep in places, there is land.

◀ This is a walrus, an Arctic seal with tusks. When out of the water walruses huddle together in their hundreds. ①

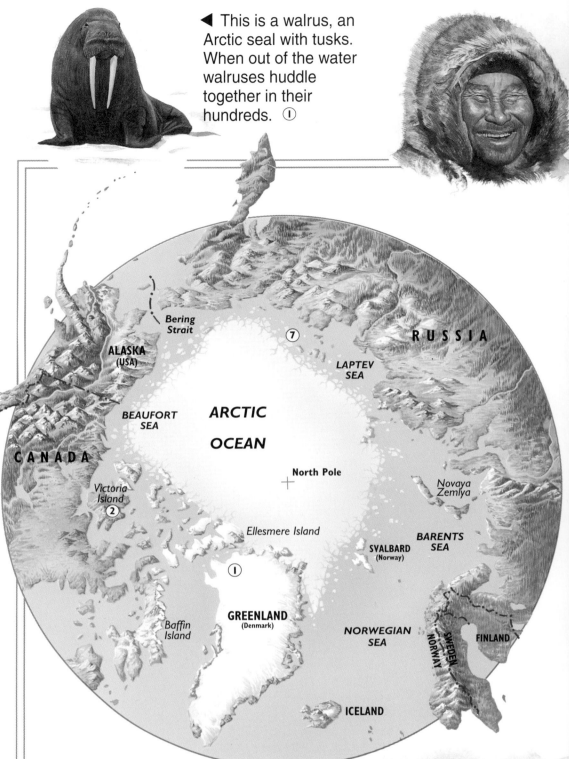

ALASKA (USA)

BEAUFORT SEA

CANADA

Victoria Island ②

Baffin Island

GREENLAND (Denmark)

Ellesmere Island ①

ARCTIC OCEAN

North Pole

Bering Strait

⑦

LAPTEV SEA

RUSSIA

Novaya Zemlya

SVALBARD (Norway)

BARENTS SEA

NORWEGIAN SEA

NORWAY

SWEDEN

FINLAND

ICELAND

▲ Ships sail through Arctic waters every day. Icebreakers carve a passage for them through the rafts of floating ice, called pack ice. ⑦

▼ Emperor penguins gather together on an Antarctic shore. (There are no penguins in the Arctic!) ⑥

◀ The Inuit, from Greenland and northern Canada, are one of many Arctic peoples who inhabit the shores of the Arctic Ocean. Some still live by hunting walruses, seals, and whales. ②

◀ The Poles were first reached by people less than one hundred years ago. An American, Robert Peary, was first to the North Pole in 1909. Norwegian explorer Roald Amundsen won a race against a British expedition led by Robert F. Scott to reach the South Pole in 1911. This picture shows a modern polar traveler. His team of husky dogs pulls his sled laden with provisions. ③

▲ The humpback whale can flip backwards right out of the water, a leap known as "breaching." The humpback is famous for its underwater singing. ④

▲ Arriving at the South Pole today, this is what you will find: an American research station. Scientists live and work here all year round. ⑤

WEDDELL SEA

QUEEN MAUD LAND

Antarctic Peninsula

ANTARCTICA

BELLINGSHAUSEN SEA

South Pole ③ ⑤

BYRD LAND

Ross Ice Shelf

WILKES LAND

ROSS SEA

Scale
0   500 km
0   400 mi

SOUTHERN OCEAN

④ ⑥

Picture Index

Map Index

PRINTED IN BELGIUM BY
proost
INTERNATIONAL BOOK PRODUCTION